'What is undoubtedly valuable about the book is the way that it carefully arranges, in a beautifully printed hardback, a selection of concrete poetry's keystones. The first half of Perloff's selection triangulates Brazil, Austria and Scotland through the work of three key figures: Augusto de Campos, Gerhard Rühm and Ian Hamilton Finlay. For the anglophone reader, she glosses the foreign words involved, prising apart the heavy punning that sparked the concrete imagination.' – Jeremy Noel-Tod, *TLS*

'This is an exciting and engaging summary of an important and still misunderstood field, the value of which lies in the intelligence and sensitivity of Perloff's close readings.' – *Burlington Contemporary*

'This is a handsome volume which radiates weightless calm and clarity. Perloff is at pains to encourage us to give the works in the book our full attention, to avoid hastily construing them as trivial word games, and she is absolutely right to do so.' – *Art Monthly*

'Perloff's new anthology presents a wide sampling of what is known as concrete poetry. Through the book's rich introduction to the nearly 200 color and black-and-white illustrations and the commentary below each, readers learn much about this postmodernist poetic genre. Perloff's book grew out of her experience as an art curator, in particular a London exhibit she curated in 2017. The book reflects the international character of this art form . . . These poems are primarily understood as art objects in and by themselves, stripped of "meaning" and narrative or lyric impulse. As promised in the introduction, readers see "visually and sonically compelling" poems. . . . Recommended.' – *Choice*

'Most of the poems in *Concrete Poetry* fill a full page (and sometimes two). Under each is Perloff's critical gloss, never more than a few sentences long, and often brilliant . . . These glosses by Perloff set a new higher standard for the critical reading of avant-garde poetry, whether concrete or visual. The two pioneering critics of avant-garde poetry, Dick Higgins and Bob Grumman, would have loved them, as do I.' – *Rain Taxi Review of Books*

T0343621

'Beautifully produced . . . Whether you leap in and buy it or consult a library copy I think its well worth your time. A book for poets, readers and art lovers. Your own formally composed verses, on the still white page, ought to be ruffled, alarmed, and if not fully converted, at least have the "look" of them excitingly challenged.' – *The High Window Review*

'Nancy Perloff's *Concrete Poetry: A 21st-Century Anthology* offers a present-day perspective on the concrete poetry movement of the 1950s through to the 1970s. The curator takes us back to that defining period, which most scholars identify as the heyday of concretism, with the aim of establishing a sort of "canon" of the most interesting and enduring contributors to the movement. Here is a body of work . . . which deserves a wider audience and greater critical attention.' – *Fortnightly Review*

'This wonderfully rich anthology reveals the experimentation and internationalism of concrete poetry and its continuing significance. Nancy Perloff's fresh selection, including the work of poets from Austria and Japan, offers scholarly insight alongside helpful notes to each poem.' – Andrew Nairne OBE, Director, Kettle's Yard, University of Cambridge

'This new anthology is to be welcomed. It features a wide range of international poets who contributed to the movement, and displays prime examples of their poetic output in its original setting. Nancy Perloff offers personal commentaries on the individual poems, and provides a historical introduction which also conveys her belief in the enduring legacy of the movement.' – Stephen Bann CBE, Emeritus Professor of History of Art, University of Bristol, and editor of *Concrete Poetry: An International Anthology* (1967)

'Perloff's lively style and tone in this book help to give new life to old forms, conveying something of the sense of adventure felt among those of us still young enough to remember being part of this post-war cultural movement. Written in a highly accessible way, with a fine choice of accompanying poems, it's a book to generate new interest as well as to inform existing initiates.' – Hansjörg Mayer, poet, typographer and publisher

# CONCRETE POETRY

## A 21st-century Anthology

Edited by Nancy Perloff

REAKTION BOOKS

Published by
REAKTION BOOKS LTD
Unit 32, Waterside
44–48 Wharf Road
London N1 7UX, UK

www.reaktionbooks.co.uk

First published 2021
Paperback edition first published 2023
Copyright © Nancy Perloff 2021

Printed and bound in India by Replika Press Pvt. Ltd

A catalogue record for this book is available from the British Library

ISBN  978 1 78914 776 6

# CONTENTS

## AUTHOR'S NOTE

With a few exceptions, this anthology does not identify the collection in which a given poem was first published. This decision has been made for the sake of consistency. Many poems appeared in multiple collections and periodicals, and it is not possible or even accurate to name an 'original' source. The editor therefore cites source collections only where they are specifically referenced in the commentaries.

# PREFACE

This anthology had its origin in an exhibition I curated on concrete poetry for the Getty Research Institute in 2017. Michael Leaman of Reaktion Books in London heard about the exhibition from colleagues and contacted me with the proposal to produce a new anthology of concrete poetry for the twenty-first century.

At first I was somewhat hesitant: over the years, there have been a number of fine anthologies of concrete poetry. These are mostly surveys, mapping the parameters of the movement in broad, general strokes. But since, as I learned from the response to my exhibition, concrete poetry remains largely unknown, it seemed high time to produce a more selective anthology for a broader public – an anthology that would underscore what I consider to be the real strengths of the movement. Earlier anthologies of concrete poetry, I should note, were principally overviews, produced by the concrete poets themselves. Mine is the first retrospective anthology, dedicated to singling out the most distinctive and significant works of this interdisciplinary and influential movement.

This book is thus a more personal response to concrete poetry. I make no attempt to provide coverage of what is a very large field. Diversity comes in many forms, and my emphasis has been, not on gender or geography, but on those constellations like the little known Wiener Gruppe and the Japanese concretists – groups that, together with the foundational Brazilians and the Scottish poet Ian Hamilton Finlay, have emphasized the most subtle possibilities of language itself. The pages that follow represent my choices of the poets I thought were most interesting and significant.

This anthology differs from earlier ones in providing individual poems with their own adjacent commentaries. My hope is that the reader will discover the intricacy of poems that have sometimes been dismissed as simple, even trivial texts. 'Viva vaia' – what makes this little poem so memorable and so unique?

# INTRODUCTION

In July 2016 I travelled to São Paulo to see a major retrospective of the art and poetry of the Brazilian concrete poet Augusto de Campos (b. 1931). Entitled *Rever* (To See Again), after a palindromic poem that Augusto first wrote in 1964, the exhibition was stunning in its colour, scale and synaesthesia.[1] Wherever I walked in the space of SESC Pompéia, a former factory converted into a leisure centre and designed by the Brazilian architect Lina Bo Bardi,[2] I encountered poetry in countless forms – as printed pages, as screenprints, in journals, as folding cards, as part of three-dimensional reliefs, in free-standing sculptures. Perhaps most contemporary were the digital projections of poetry on the walls. Here, the motion of different, often coloured fonts coincided with the mesmerizing voices of Augusto and his son Cid Campos, and of the singer, composer and songwriter Caetano Veloso. Evocative shapes such as the billowing black hole rimmed by yellow in 'sos' and the rushing catapult of word roots in 'Cidade/City/Cité' infused speed into the space and introduced new electronic sounds, enhancing the close relation of the verbal, the vocal and the visual in Augusto's work and demonstrating both his pursuit of multimedia and his sophisticated application of technology to poetry.

I introduce this anthology with the exhibition *Rever* because Augusto's concrete poetry, as here displayed, belongs to a large corpus of visually evocative work by poets who have been curiously overlooked in the Anglophone world of the twenty-first century. To determine why, one must first answer the question, 'What is – or was – *concrete poetry*?' This is a surprisingly difficult question. The term 'concrete poetry' refers both to a poetic genre and to the international movement that first emerged in Brazil and Austria in the early 1950s. Concrete poetry must be distinguished from visual poetry, a more general term for poems that focus primarily on the visual arrangement of language. Unlike concrete poetry, visual poetry can refer to a history as old as writing itself. In Johanna Drucker's words, 'Certainly the scribes who incised Egyptian hieroglyphics into the material substrate of walls and sarcophagi from about 2700 BC onward were sensitive to the visual arrangement of their signs.'[3]

But today we understand visual poetry as a larger category that subsumes concretism. Indeed, some critics make the historical argument that the concrete poetry movement, so important in Europe, the United Kingdom and Asia from the 1950s until the 1970s, charted the territory for the visual poetry that followed it, even as concrete poetry itself fell away. An essential principle of concretism – 'that language has a visual dimension and that the actual "look" of a poem on the page determines, at least in part, its meaning' – became central to visual poetics as practised in the late twentieth century and today.[4] Typewriter art, a subset of visual poetry, creates images composed of brackets, dashes, slashes and asterisks, as well as other forms of graphic art, all by manipulating the keyboard and the typewriter roller. The early work of the Finnish-Swedish artist and poet Cia Rinne illustrates this practice.

How then to differentiate between the genres of visual and concrete poetry? I would argue that visual poetry departs from concrete poetry in its tendency to combine typewriter text with imagery and computer graphics, in its lack of concern with formal simplification and reduction, and in the self-identification of gallery-based artists as 'visual poets'. Kenneth Goldsmith lauds the intersection of technology with the work of visual poets who 'plaster gallery walls with word decals, pump out poster-sized broadsides, tap out smartphone poetry, and publish print-on-demand books of poetry'.[5] Another central difference, noted by Augusto de Campos, between concrete and visual poetry is concrete's placement of semantic values on an equal footing with the material, visual and sonorous parameters of the poem.[6] Certainly

not all visual poetry is concrete poetry, since not all of the former embraces what James Joyce called the 'verbivocovisual'. In a given concrete poem or 'constellation', the visual, sonic and semantic dimensions of a poem cannot be separated: form equals meaning.

At the opposite end of the spectrum from visual poetry lies the genre of sound poetry, which alters the characteristic relationship between sound and sense by 'multiplying, reducing, or denying semantic reference, while expanding the phonetic and aural properties of language'.[7] Although sound poetry has been present throughout the history of Western literature and has origins in the vast array of poetry, chant structures and syllabic mouthings still alive among many North American, African, Asian and Oceanic peoples, its immediate origins can be traced to the international network of the European avant-gardes.[8]

The Russian Futurists, to take the earliest example, wrote their poetry in the language of *zaum*, a neologism built from the preposition *za* (beyond) and the noun *um* (the mind) and best translated as 'beyonsense'. Placing a primacy on 'the word as such' and on 'sound as such', the Futurist poets Aleksei Kruchenykh and Velimir Khlebnikov conveyed in their manifestos that 'beyonsense' words are phonic, and that this phonic dimension itself becomes the content. *Zaum* poetry derived its meaning from phonetic analogies: the neologisms *mechari* (swordsmen) and *smekhiri* (laughers) shared more in common than *mechari* with *gladiatory* (gladiators), because 'it is the phonetic composition of the word which gives it its living coloration.'[9] Such sonic affinities, moreover, can generate new meanings. Among the historical avant-gardes, the sound poetry of the Italian Futurists explored *parole-in-libertà* (words-in-freedom), which abolished syntax and punctuation and utilized evocative onomatopoeia. For example, sonic connections between syllables like 'traac craac' convey a mimetic suggestion of machines.[10] German Dadaists working with sound poetry in the 1920s dispensed with semantic units altogether and explored sound for its abstract and musical qualities.

Like concrete poetry, sound poetry is a hybrid form working across media. Yet an effective analysis of a sound poem's text, as opposed to that of a concrete poem, must consider its realization in live performance and hence the very nature of its *sounds* – their intelligibility, their relation to other sounds in the poem, their use of the pronunciation of a particular spoken language, their role in articulating structure. Sound poetry does not privilege meaning, and in performance we hear its probing of the limits of referentiality.[11]

In 1930, in his 'Manifesto for Concrete Art', the Dutch artist and theorist Theo van Doesburg formulated the term 'concrete art' in order to advocate the building up of painting with purely plastic elements (surfaces and colours) that exclude lyricism, drama and symbolism. Max Bill, Swiss theorist and painter, followed van Doesburg in the pursuit of a concrete art that influenced concrete poetry through its rejection of subjectivity and emotion. Although Brazilian concrete poetry officially launched at the First National Exhibition of Concrete Art at the Museu de Arte Moderna of São Paulo in 1956, it had already assumed an independent voice by championing the 'verbivocovisual'.

All the poets in this anthology would no doubt agree with Rosmarie Waldrop's basic definition, 'Concrete poetry is a revolt against the transparency of the word.' And it 'is a poetry that makes the sound and shape of words its explicit field of investigation'.[12] But, beyond such basics, what have been the defining features of concrete as put forth by the poets themselves?

## Sweden: The First Manifesto

Contemporary definitions such as Waldrop's build on the writings of the 1950s, when several concrete poets wrote manifestos introducing the new poetic genre. The Brazilian-born Swedish poet Öyvind Fahlström published the first manifesto in 1953 (when he was 25 years old) and entitled it *Hipy papy bthuthdththuthda bthuthdy.* He found the inspiration for his title in a Swedish translation of Owl's attempt at writing 'A happy birthday' in A. A. Milne's *Winnie-the-Pooh*.[13] Fahlström added the subtitle 'Manifesto for Concrete Poetry', and when he reprinted the text in 1966 he made some minor deletions. His manifesto begins with two epigraphs: the first calls for a shift from lyric poetry to writing 'worlets' (words, letters); the second uses a quotation in French from F. T. Marinetti's *Technical Manifesto of Futurist Literature* (1912) – 'Remplacer la psychologie de l'homme . . . par L'OBSESSION LYRIQUE DE LA MATIÈRE' – in which the

Öyvind Fahlström, 1960.

Italian poet advocates the destruction of syntax, adjectives, adverbs and all verb forms except the infinitive, and of punctuation, in favour of 'tight networks of analogies' between disparate images.[14] Marinetti's call to replace the lyric 'I' with *matter* – noise, weight and smell – finds its way into Fahlström's manifesto in statements such as: 'Poetry is not only for analysis; it is also structure. Not just structure with the emphasis on expression of ideas, but also concrete structure.'

The attention to matter likewise figures prominently in Fahlström's imperative to 'KNEAD the linguistic material; this is what justifies the label concrete. Don't just manipulate the whole structure; begin rather with the smallest elements – letters, words.' Fahlström uses the example of concrete music (*musique concrète*) to offer his unique perspective on concrete poetry. He emphasizes reduction, as with his 'worlets':

The fundamental principle of concrete poetry is perhaps most beautifully illustrated by Pierre Schaeffer's experience

during his search for concrete music . . . he cut out a small
fragment of railway engine sound and repeated this fragment
at a slightly different pitch; then went back to the first, then
the second, and so on, setting up an alternation. Only then
had he actually created; he has operated on the material itself
by cutting it up; the elements were not new; but from the new
context thereby created emerged new matter.[15]

Fahlström's manifesto represents his most direct intervention
in the concrete poetry movement. Following its publication, his
career moved in a different direction. He became more interested
in *musique concrète*, as is already evident in the passage above,
and explored radio as a medium in which he could overlay the
same word, record text backwards and then reverse the tape, and
insert words that he read out in different acoustic settings (room
sounds).[16] Abroad, his manifesto went unnoticed until 1968, when
it appeared in an English translation for the first time in Mary Ellen
Solt's *Concrete Poetry: A World View* (translated from Swedish by
Solt and Karen Loevgren). Its prescience, however, must be taken
into account. As we will see in addressing subsequent manifestos by
the Bolivian-born Swiss poet Eugen Gomringer and the Brazilians
Augusto and Haroldo de Campos, Fahlström anticipated their
theories of language, concrete structure and materiality without
having been in touch with them prior to writing his manifesto. As
he remarked, 'I hadn't heard of the Brazilians although I was born
in Brazil. The trouble is I don't read Portuguese.'[17] While Fahlström
is an extremely important theorist of the concrete, his artwork does
not relate to his manifesto. I therefore include him here, but not in
the anthology itself.

## Gomringer: *From Line to Constellation*

In 1955, two years after the publication of Fahlström's manifesto,
Gomringer wrote his own manifesto, which he called *From Line
to Constellation*. Gomringer was working at the time as secretary
to Max Bill, director of the Hochschule für Gestaltung in Ulm,
Germany. He was not familiar with the contemporary poetics
of Fahlström or the Brazilians. Rather, concrete art, with its

emphasis on line, surface and colour and its geometric abstraction, guided Gomringer during a period in which he had ceased writing sonnets (1950) but had not yet discovered a new form of poetry. The concrete art promoted by Max Bill looked back to the 1930 'Manifesto for Concrete Art' of van Doesburg, which argued that 'a pictorial element does not have any meaning beyond itself.' Gomringer attended the international exhibition of concrete art in Basel, organized by Bill in 1944; met Bill and fellow painters Richard Paul Lohse and Camille Graeser at the Galerie des Eaux Vives, a special gallery for concrete painting, in Zürich in 1944–5; and in Berne in 1951 joined his friends the graphic artists Dieter Roth and Marcel Wyss in their plan to publish a magazine called *Spirale*, which would embrace poetry, the plastic arts, graphics, architecture and industrial design.[18] This exposure helps to explain why Gomringer repeatedly emphasized the influence of concrete art on his poetic work.

When Gomringer first started writing concrete poetry, he called his poems 'constellations', a term he borrowed from the French Symbolist poet Stéphane Mallarmé. Gomringer was probably thinking specifically of Mallarmé's experimental poem *Un coup de dés jamais n'abolira le hasard* (A Throw of the Dice Will Never Abolish Chance, 1897), with its introduction of a typography and page design capable of expressing movement in space and time. Gomringer published his first book of poetry, *Constellations*, in 1953. His manifesto, *From Line to Constellation*, alludes to the transition he himself had experienced from the poetic line – a verse read in one line or sequentially, like a sonnet – to visual poems or 'constellations':

> So the new poem is simple and can be perceived visually as a whole as well as in its parts. It becomes an object to be both seen and used: an object containing thought but made concrete through play-activity, its concern is with brevity and conciseness.[19]

Indeed, 'concentration and simplification' were the essence of Gomringer's concrete poetry. He concluded his manifesto by presenting and defining his concept of the 'constellation':

The constellation is the simplest possible kind of configuration in poetry which has for its basic unit the word, it encloses a group of words as if it were drawing stars together to form a cluster . . . In the constellation something is brought into the world. It is a reality in itself and not a poem about something or other.[20]

In two subsequent manifestos, *Max Bill and Concrete Poetry* (1958) and *The Poem as a Functional Object* (1960), Gomringer advocates preparing concrete poetry for its 'use of the elements of language – with the word as a totality' and characterizes concrete poetry as a 'conscious study of the material and its structure . . . material means the sum of all the signs with which we make poems'.[21] Thus Fahlström and Gomringer independently addressed similar attributes of the new poetry and did so during the same years: 1953 and 1954. For his theoretical writing, his constellations such as 'Silencio', 'Ping Pong' and 'Wind', and his editing of *Spirale, Konkrete Poesie Poesia Concreta* and other anthologies, Gomringer has come to be considered the father of concrete poetry in the German-speaking world.

## Brazil: Augusto de Campos and Noigandres

The Brazilian poets developed a close relationship with Gomringer during the early years of their movement, then shifted away towards an incorporation of modernism and new technology. Indeed, Haroldo de Campos, brother of Augusto, offered the following critique in an essay published in his collection *Novas*:

Brazilian concrete poetry, for its critics and observers (and also, clearly, for its opponents) seemed irrevocably baroque, pluralist, multifaceted, in comparison with the austere orthogonality of Gomringer's *Konstellationen*, pure and clear, like a composition by Max Bill. Our 'difference' produced a varying result in the chemistry of the poem, even if the global content of the new poetic program had common points.[22]

It will be interesting to see how 'difference' between the 'baroque' and the 'orthogonal' plays out in examples in this anthology of

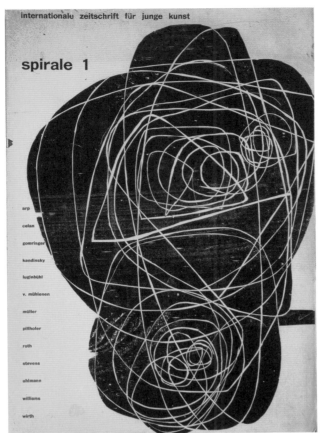

*Spirale: internationale Zeitschrift für junge Kunst*, 1, cover, woodcut by Dieter Roth, 1952.

the concrete poetry of Augusto and Haroldo and Gomringer's constellations. The two brothers met Décio Pignatari in the late 1940s at the University of São Paulo Law Faculty. Sharing an interest in poetry, they founded the group they called 'Noigandres' in 1952. The complex etymology of the name is prophetic, as the three poets went on to pursue layered and intricate puns, anagrams and portmanteau words in their work. Borrowed from 'Canto xx' by Ezra Pound, the word 'noigandres' can be traced to the great troubadour poet Arnaut Daniel and to the Provençal scholar Emil Lévy, who puzzled over its meaning ('Noigandres! Eh noigandres! Now what the DEFFIL can that mean!') until he discovered that it should be divided in two and translated as follows: *enoi* (ennui) and *gandres*, from *gandir* (to ward off, remove).[23]

Like Gomringer, the Noigandres poets participated in developments in the visual arts as well as in poetry. In Brazil they

*Konkrete Poesie Poesia Concreta*, 1, cover, edited by
Eugen Gomringer, 1960.

were in contact with the Ruptura group, which organized its first
exhibition of concrete art at the São Paulo Museum of Modern
Art in 1952 and included poster-poems by the Noigandres group.
The techniques of poetry construction of Mallarmé, Pound, e. e.
cummings and Joyce inspired the linguistic experiments of
Noigandres.[24] Between 1952 and 1958 they published five issues of

Haroldo de Campos, Décio Pignatari, Augusto de Campos (left to right) in São Paulo, 1952.

the journal to which they lent their name, each containing selections of their poetry and prose. The first issue featured a colourful cover by Pignatari displaying the cursive letters N O I G A N D R, while the second and fourth issues contained contributions of particular significance for the group.

The second issue (1955) featured the first printing of Augusto's collection of poetry *Poetamenos* (Minuspoet), completed in 1953 and, to quote from his preface, 'aspiring to the hope of a KLANGFARBENMELODIE with words'. He modelled this method, best translated as a 'melody of tone colours', on the Viennese avant-garde composer Anton Webern, who created a 'continuous melody dislocating from one instrument to another, constantly changing its color'. Augusto applied this technique to poetry by pursuing an analogy between musical instruments and components of language – 'phrase / word / syllable / letter (s)' – whose timbres he defined by a 'graphic-phonetic' or 'ideogrammic' theme.[25] Coloured fonts in the poetry highlight semantic and phonetic relationships. Moreover, Augusto explicitly calls for 'oral reading', in which human voices act as timbres for the poem, like the instruments in Webern's *Klangfarbenmelodie*. *Poetamenos* marked the arrival of concrete poetry in Brazil and the first major contribution of Augusto de Campos.[26]

Augusto completed his *Poetamenos* the same year that Gomringer published his *Constellations* and Fahlström wrote his manifesto for concrete poetry. The beginning of the international concrete poetry movement can thus be traced back as early as 1953.[27] In 1955, while travelling in Europe, Décio Pignatari visited the Hochschule in Ulm and met Gomringer for the first time. The two poets exchanged publications (*Constellations* and *Noigandres* no. 2), and Gomringer published some of the Brazilian poems in

*Noigandres*, 1, cover by Décio Pignatari, 1952.

*Spirale*. The meeting, as later recounted by Augusto, was pivotal
in establishing the term 'concrete poetry', which had originated
with the Brazilians and the Ruptura group.[28] In a letter he wrote
to Pignatari around the time of the concrete art exhibition in São
Paulo (when Pignatari was still in Europe), Augusto argued that the
term 'concrete poetry' 'might better characterize our position than

the word "ideogram'". He also quoted from a letter (in French) that Gomringer sent to Pignatari in 1956 upon his return to São Paulo:

> votre titre 'poésie concrète' me plâit très bien. Avant de nommer mes 'poèmes' constellations j'avais vraiment pensé de les nommer 'concrètes'. On pourrait bien nommer toute l'anthologie 'poésie concrète', quant à moi.[29]

> your title 'concrete poetry' pleases me very much. Before calling my 'poems' constellations I had truly thought of calling them 'concrete'. One could certainly call the entire anthology 'concrete poetry', as far as I'm concerned.

In 1960, following up perhaps on this letter, Gomringer published a 'Kleine Anthologie konkreter Poesie' (Short Anthology of Concrete Poetry) as an additional text to *Spirale* no. 8, bringing together sixteen poets, seven of whom were Brazilian.

The fourth issue of *Noigandres* appeared in 1958 in a format suitable for housing the loose poster-poems within. Typeset entirely in the Futura font, the poems suggest industrial reproducibility, thus echoing and reinforcing the plans underway by architect and urban planner Lúcio Costa to construct the new Brazilian capital, Brasília. With their poster-poems, the Noigandres poets published their jointly authored manifesto *Plano piloto para poesia concreta* (Pilot Plan for Concrete Poetry), in which they articulated their definition of concrete poetry. The language of the Pilot Plan is technical, abbreviated, telegraphic and influenced by cybernetics.[30] Its opening paragraph contains the following statement:

> concrete poetry begins by being aware of graphic space as structural agent. qualified space: space-time structure instead of mere linear-temporistical development. hence the importance of ideogram concept, either in its general sense of spatial or visual syntax, or in its specific sense (fenollosa/ pound) of method of composition based on direct – analogical, not logical-discursive – juxtaposition of elements.

*Noigandres*, 4, cover by Hermelindo Fiaminghi, 1958.

Although Fahlström never knew the Noigandres group, the Swedish poet's emphasis on concrete structure, matter, reduction and analogies between disparate images, and his rejection of the lyric subject and linear discourse, resurface in intriguing ways, if expressed in an entirely different language and vision, in the work of the Brazilians. Moreover, the Pilot Plan keeps returning to definitions, resulting in multiple investigations of terminology. For instance (to continue):

> concrete poetry: tension of things-words in space-time . . . and so in music – by definition, a time art – space intervenes (webern and his followers . . . concrete and electronic music); in visual arts – spatial by definition – time intervenes (mondrian . . . max bill . . . concrete art in general).

And the poets address the equivalence of form and meaning, as well as the interdisciplinary role of concrete poetry, in the following terms:

> concrete poem communicates its own structure: structure-content. concrete poem is an object in and by itself, not an interpreter of exterior objects and/or more or less subjective feelings. its material: the word (sound, visual form, semantical charge) . . . concrete poem . . . creates a specific linguistical area – 'verbivocovisual' –, which shares the advantages of non-verbal communication, without giving up words' virtualities.[31]

In an article written one year earlier and entitled 'Concrete Poetry – Language – Communication', Haroldo de Campos argued that

> the concrete poem does not communicate an outer message and content, but rather it uses these resources to communicate forms, to create and corroborate, verbivocovisually, a content-structure . . . the concrete poet's task will be the creation of forms, of artistic content-structures whose material is the word.

Contemporary critiques that argue concrete poetry is asemantic thus fall short, as Haroldo demonstrates in his comprehensive and profound reading of Pignatari's poem 'Terra'.[32]

## Austria: Gerhard Rühm and the Wiener Gruppe

While the contributions of the Brazilian poets have been discussed in earlier anthologies such as Mary Ellen Solt's, the role of Austrian concrete poetry remains almost unknown in the Anglophone world. One might speculate that this is because the Austrians did not seek to promote their work abroad and lacked the Brazilians' fluency in English (with the exception of Ernst Jandl). Moreover, most concrete poets did not speak or read German and tended to associate it negatively with the Second World War. The Wiener Gruppe (Vienna Group) began to coalesce in 1952 as a circle of friends. In 1950 the poet Hans Carl Artmann and the composer Gerhard Rühm emerged on the Vienna art scene. Konrad Bayer joined them in 1952, and through him in 1953 the jazz musician Oswald Wiener, who began writing poetry in 1954. The architect Friedrich Achleitner joined in 1955. As a group, they staged literary cabarets ('happenings' *avant la lettre*) on 6 December 1958 and 15 April 1959, participated in the 'artclub' (a venue for new artistic developments), wrote and produced plays, operettas and songs, and organized poetry readings.[33] They remained active as a group from 1954 to 1960.[34]

Rühm, the group's spokesperson, has since pursued a career as a sound poet, concrete poet, 'typo-collagist', draughtsman and composer to the present day.[35] Interestingly, unlike Fahlström, Gomringer and the Brazilian concretists, he did not write manifestos. Yet his two major texts on the Vienna Group (1967) and on 'konkrete poesie' capture his distinctive concept of the concrete poetry movement and its practice. Using the terms 'constellations' and 'concrete poetry' somewhat interchangeably, Rühm defines both as

> a kind of 'isolated' poetry, in which the individual words gained independence. In the attempt to objectify and reduce the 'poem' as much as possible to the totality of the individual term (because the mere confrontation with another one limits its spectrum of associations) I ended up, in extreme cases, with 'one-word tablets', giving up the hierarchic principle of the sentence in order to rid words from their commitment to conveying meaning and to make them available as elements of

Gerhard Rühm, Second Literary Cabaret, Vienna, 1959.

> equal value . . . the differentiation between contents and form
> is no longer valid: putting something in a slightly different
> place lends it a different meaning.[36]

Components of Rühm's definition here – one-word poems, the
axiom that 'form equals content', the departure from normal
syntax – recall the theories of Fahlström and the Noigandres
poets. Moreover, Rühm recounts that he and Achleitner had the
opportunity to meet Gomringer in Ulm in summer 1956, close
to the time of Pignatari's visit. He describes their meeting as the
first 'with like-minded persons abroad'. And he credits Gomringer
with being the theoretical founder of concrete poetry and the
Noigandres group with shaping it.[37]

Yet real differences distinguish Rühm from his Swiss and
Brazilian colleagues, most significantly his focus on the sound of
concrete poetry. Perhaps he chose not to write a manifesto because
he did not want to be considered exclusively a 'concrete poet'. His
two extensive essays utilize multiple designations for his poetry:
'word and sound designs', 'dialect poems (foreign words, remote
languages)', the *Klanggestalt* (soundshape) of speech versus the
*Schriftbild* (writingpicture). Rühm summarizes these considerations

as follows:

in no way is all 'concrete poetry', as is often assumed, 'visual poetry' – a meaningful part is conceived as auditory, that means: it has to do with poetic texts which are intended to be heard, to activate musical parameters of language.[38]

At the same time, Rühm accentuates 'visualization' as an essential component of concrete poetry. It brings an additional piece of information not contained in the text, he argues. Hence the word 'ideogram' rather than 'calligram'.[39] Encountering Rühm's concrete poetry reveals that he did indeed emphasize the visual and could therefore have applied the 'verbivocovisual' principle of the Brazilians, even though this is not a term we see him use. Yet Rühm's visual arrangements of typewritten letters and words tend to reinforce the play of the sonic, which he uses to generate layered meanings and new forms of language.

## Scotland: Ian Hamilton Finlay

The Scottish poet Ian Hamilton Finlay did not start writing concrete poems until 1963. He spent the first part of this decade educating himself both in the 1950s work of fellow concretists and in modern poetry. Enjoying a close friendship with the Austrian sound poet Ernst Jandl, Finlay wrote on 30 September 1965: 'I was very pleased you showed my poems to Gerhardt [sic] Ruhm . . . What sort of thing is G. Ruhm doing now, I'd be awfully interested to know. I like his work a lot.'[40]

In addition to his interest in the work of Jandl and Rühm, Finlay had a brief but intense correspondence with Augusto de Campos, in which he played the role of pupil and Augusto of mentor.[41] In April 1963, for instance, Finlay sent Augusto what he referred to as his 'formal poem', which would become part of the collection called *Rapel*. He wished to solicit Augusto's opinion and, in addition, to request a Portuguese/English dictionary ('money is so short . . . You will PLEASE not think I am rude . . .'), as well as a rough English translation of Mallarmé's *Un coup de dés jamais n'abolira le hasard*.[42] Augusto replied (on 1 May 1963) by praising the 'formal poem' for its 'pure movement' and its final palindromic reading, which is 'maybe the best you did. I think the more concrete

Ian Hamilton Finlay with *Ring of Waves* plexiglass sculpture, 1969.

are the poems where less a story is implied, where they are not *about* something but simply are.'

Augusto calls *Un coup de dés* 'THE basic poem', but says he is not able to translate it.[43] In a letter of 30 June 1963, he sends Finlay a portion of his English translation of the poem's definitive 1914 edition, prefaced by the remarks that he feels unable to translate it into English or into Portuguese, because this constellation of words with its 'prismatic subdivisions of thought', as Mallarmé called it, is 'so difficult and at the same time so precise'.[44] Augusto does assume responsibility for introducing Finlay to the work of other artists and poets of the European avant-garde, namely a sound poem by Theo van Doesburg, 'Voorbijtrekkende Troep' (Marching Troop, 1916), and a visual poem by the German poet Christian Morgenstern, 'Fisches Nachtgesang' (The Night Song of the Fishes), written in 1905 and published in László Moholy-Nagy's *Vision in Motion* (1947). In his letter, Augusto also provides Moholy-Nagy's commentary:

> 'The Night Song of the Fishes' is a visual joke. The arc and dash signs of the poetical foot are used here partly to indicate the rhythmic structure of the mute poem and partly to characterize the opening and the closing of the fishes' mouths when swimming.

To this, Augusto adds: 'And maybe fish scales, too?'[45]

Like Rühm, Finlay did not write manifestos. Rather, he used the occasion of letter-writing to forge connections and, during the 1960s, to discuss his work and test his theories of language and concrete poetry. An important correspondence with the American concrete poet Emmett Williams began in June 1963 when Finlay wrote to him out of the blue, having secured Williams's address from the poet Jerome Rothenberg. Finlay immediately engaged Williams with his principal concern: concrete poetry. In the following very thoughtful and revealing passage, he identifies his role in the movement and talks through what he understands 'concrete' to mean:

> Would appreciate it if we could be in touch about concrete poetry . . . Very difficult in Scotland to know what is going on in other places. And lonely, and so on. Maybe you could write a few lines about your idea of concrete? And maybe type a couple of poems for me to see? . . . I don't know what the world is doing about concrete; as a matter of fact I thought I had invented it . . . Then I came in contact with Augusto de Campos, so I know about concrete in Brazil, and I like their stuff enormously . . . Well! It seems like concrete is really many things, not one way at all. Myself, I got to it, precariously, which is how I ever get anywhere, by having huge worries about what I call syntax, or movement maybe . . . I found myself wanting to slow it down, and even stop it, so the words could be left at a halt – i.e. syntax seem to function as a forward movement, and on another level, if you extend this movement, as a line, far enough, you end up in social being, and I wanted something purer – purer, and about things, and without the word 'I', and with nouns rather than adjectives.

A bit later Finlay concludes, in words nearly identical to Augusto's in his comment on the 'formal poem': 'Maybe I would better say, concrete is non-didactic – didactic, the saying ABOUT, is over.'[46]

## The Recovery of the Early Avant-garde

From Fahlström to Finlay (1950s–60s), definitions of concrete poetry are varied and nuanced, yet revolve around similar principles: language as material; form (the visual, sonic, semantic dimensions of words) equals content ('content-structure'); rejection of the lyric 'I'; reduction to a small number of words; the pursuit of the 'verbivocovisual'. In a letter to Jandl, Finlay expressed much of this concisely: 'The notion that "something to say" is actually a *modulation of the material* scarcely enters anyone's head.'[47]

The convergence of definitions raises a provocative question: why did similar ideas emerge in such different geographic locations in the 1950s? Augusto de Campos and Gerhard Rühm are in agreement about the answer: the need, in the post-war years, to rediscover the early avant-garde. Augusto enacts this revival by introducing Finlay to early sound and visual poetry (Theo van Doesburg, Christian Morgenstern, Hugo Ball) and by translating Mallarmé. He articulates the broader development as follows:

> I think there was a very important demand for change, for the recovery of the avant-garde movements. We had had two great wars that marginalized, put aside for many, many years, the things that interested us. You see, the music of Webern, Schoenberg and Alban Berg, for example, was not played because it was condemned both in Germany and in Russia, the two dictatorships. You could say that all experimental poetry, all experimental art, was in a certain sense marginalized.[48]

To the Viennese musical avant-garde, Augusto added both American and European modernists whose work he not only 'recovered', but translated into Portuguese: Dante Alighieri, William Blake, John Donne, Emily Dickinson, Arthur Rimbaud, Mallarmé, Pound, Paul Valéry, Vladimir Mayakovsky and the Provençal poets.[49] Haroldo applied the term 'transcreation', based on Pound's 'criticism via translation', to the extensive translation work he too pursued.

Rühm's account of the need for recovery, which dates from 1967, is intriguingly similar to Augusto's:

> After seven years of enforced separation, there was an urgent need to recover lost ground and for us, the young ones, to rediscover modern art, especially in Austria; the big libraries had failed to collect its most important documents, or they had been purged . . . The fragmented information on

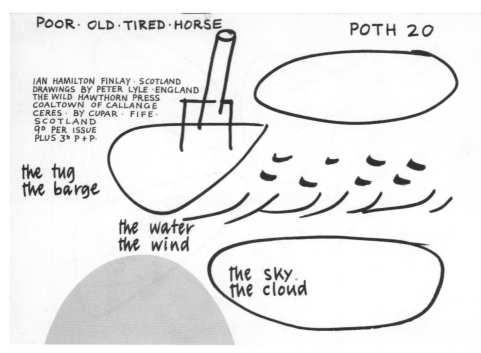

IAN HAMILTON FINLAY·SCOTLAND
DRAWINGS BY PETER LYLE·ENGLAND
THE WILD HAWTHORN PRESS
COALTOWN OF CALLANGE
CERES·BY CUPAR·FIFE·
SCOTLAND
9ᴰ PER ISSUE
PLUS 3ᴰ P + P·

the tug
the barge

the water
the wind

the sky
the cloud

*Poor.Old.Tired.Horse.*, 20, cover, 'The Tug/The Barge', co-authored by
Ian Hamilton Finlay and Peter Lyle, 1966.

expressionism, Dadaism, surrealism, constructivism, was
lapped up eagerly.[50]

Finlay displayed his commitment to rediscovering the avant-
garde through a particular affinity with Russian modernism.
His poetry sometimes comprises cerebral, semiotic readings
and visualizations of the theories of Russian Futurism and
Suprematism, specifically of *zaum* (transrational poetry), of the
'word as such' and of the abstraction and minimalism of Kazimir
Malevich's Suprematist painting. Since he spoke no Russian, Finlay
relied on the knowledge of fellow concrete poet Edwin Morgan,
who provided idiosyncratic translations often using a Scots version
of *zaum*.

The Noigandres poets likewise admired the Russian avant-
garde, especially the Constructivist El Lissitzky and the 'poet
of the Revolution', Vladimir Mayakovsky. In order to learn his
experimental poetry, they studied Russian. Moreover, they
inserted Mayakovsky's theorem 'without revolutionary form there

is no revolutionary art' at the end of their *Pilot Plan*. Even as they mastered multiple languages, Augusto and Haroldo de Campos believed in transcending nationality in order to make their poetry accessible. When Augusto published his concrete poetry in Finlay's magazine, *Poor.Old.Tired.Horse.*, whose audience was principally British and American, he provided English glossaries for the individual words.[51]

## Transnationality

Augusto's gesture suggests a provocative difference between the historical avant-gardes and the neo-avant-garde movement of concrete poetry. The early avant-gardists were largely nationalists. Language was a marker of poetic and cultural identity. Russian and Italian Futurists, for instance, vied with one another for control of the medium of the manifesto, and Russian *zaum* posed a challenge to the onomatopoeic language of the *parole-in-libertà*. Expressionism defined itself through its use of the German language, as attested to by the almanac *Der Blaue Reiter* (1912). And even in Dada, a more international movement, members such as Kurt Schwitters inserted umlauts into the score of his *Ursonate* (1922–32) so as to make sure that readers adhered to the correct German pronunciation. Similarly, the Dada poet Hugo Ball, co-founder of the Cabaret Voltaire in Zurich, intended his famous *Lautgedicht* (sound poem) 'Gadji beri bimba' (1916) to imitate the sounds of multiple languages, including, most prominently, German.

By contrast, concrete poets emphasized the 'transnationality' of their poetry. According to Rühm: 'Transnationality, a new phenomenon in literature, is an important aspect of "concrete poetry", which caters to the need for a simplified world language.'[52] Augusto associates the transcendence of linguistic boundaries with the important role that countries on the periphery (Brazil, Scotland, Austria) played in founding and leading the international concrete poetry movement:

> And the simple fact that poets of [such a] little-known
> language as Portuguese were involved in the launching of a
> movement that exceeded the frontiers of the western world

to project itself [all the way to] Japan, in the poetry of Niikuni, Takahashi and others, shows an uncommon vocation to overcome the linguistic barriers.[53]

The utopian goal of transnationality was shared by fellow concretists.[54] Moreover, Rühm noted another reason for producing 'elementary constellations out of only a few linked, solid, concrete words'. He called this practice an 'aesthetic act of purification and clarity' after the 'language desecration of the Nazi barbarians'.[55]

Yet even then, the aspiration towards a global language should not eclipse the importance, especially for certain nationalities, of pronunciation and of the sounds of a given language in conveying meaning in concrete poetry. A felicitous example would be the German language utilized by Rühm and the Wiener Gruppe and by Jandl, which contains suggestive sounds of the Viennese dialect and playful shifts in meaning depending upon context. Invented words contribute to this challenge. As Jandl noted to Finlay, his sound poems are based on the 'phonetic structure of German, a language sounding harsher than English'.[56] In Portuguese, to take another example, it is essential to read the poetry aloud to appreciate the homophones and the rhyming sounds of individual words, which sometimes acquire shared meanings and at other times highlight difference (for the latter, see Augusto's 'Sem um numero' (without a number), where 'sem' rhymes with 'cem', meaning 'one hundred' and hence the opposite).

## Why a New Anthology?

The preceding overview of poets' definitions and manifestos helps capture the multifaceted genre of concrete poetry as it might be presented in a single anthology. Concrete poetry lends itself to anthologizing, moreover, because the poems are short (generally suited to one page) and visually distinctive. Yet the question of what constitutes a *good* anthology of concrete poetry is both interesting and challenging. Today we find ourselves in a moment when we can look back at the core decades of concrete poetry – the 1950s to the 1970s – and make critical judgements about

who the leading and truly innovative poets were, how individual practitioners resembled and differed from one another, the extent to which nationality played a significant role, the continued dependence on the 'verbivocovisual', and even the relationship between theories of concrete poetry during its key decades and our understanding of the genre today.

With the benefit of time, a new anthology can make an important statement through its selection and organization of the poetry. In addition, such an anthology can contribute critical and scholarly commentary on each poem, opening a window on to how to read concrete poetry and how to explicate the subtleties of its language and its visual and semantic density. Concrete poetry often looks easy, playful and accessible – think of Finlay's 'To the Painter Jean Gris', Augusto's 'Viva vaia' or Rühm's 'Leer/Lärm' – but it is often difficult to understand. The minimalist language, consisting sometimes of only one or two words, poses a challenge for analysis. Moreover, a productive analysis needs to consider not only the shape but the sonic and the verbal components of the language. In this anthology, I have introduced my own commentaries (as opposed to those of the poets), and I have selected poets and poems based on my own criteria. I therefore call this a revisionary anthology. I will explain my selections in the final section of this Introduction. First, a word on previous anthologies.

In the late 1960s, when concretism was still new and active and therefore not quite ripe for critical assessment, four anthologies were published. The art historian Stephen Bann, the concrete poet and Fluxus artist Emmett Williams, the editor of the *Chicago Review* Eugene Wildman and the poet, translator, editor and essayist Mary Ellen Solt each produced their anthologies between 1967 and 1968.[57] The anthologies resemble one another in taking an encyclopaedic approach and in treating concrete poetry as a new phenomenon – a new kind of poetry. Commentary, where included, consists of excerpts from the poets' own writings. Bann and Solt contribute expansive introductions. Bann's reflects his deep scholarship in the field and his special friendship with Finlay, whose poetry he wrote about extensively, highlighting its philosophical and historical dimensions. Solt's offers both valuable surveys of the poetry in each country and translations of the major manifestos, some appearing in English for the first time. Solt set the

Mary Ellen Solt, c. 1980.

stage; without her anthology, we would not know the genre. Since hers was the first major anthology of concrete poetry, she inevitably sought for inclusiveness and breadth; half a century later we can now discriminate between the more and less important of these many poets and perspectives.

Since the 1960s, one significant English-language anthology has been published. Edited by Alex Balgiu and Mónica de la Torre and entitled *Women in Concrete Poetry: 1959–1979*, this new volume attests to the importance of concrete poetry today. Focused on highlighting the role of fifty women, the editors consider the label 'concrete poetry' as limiting. Like many of the poets featured in their book, they might prefer a term such as 'word-based art'. The principle that form equals meaning in a concrete poem is no longer a criterion, since the concern for Balgiu and de la Torre has shifted to the 'activation of language in public space'.[58] Social and political concerns thus supersede notions of meaning based on the 'sound and shape of words', to echo Rosmarie Waldrop's definition of concrete poetry. Some of the poets in *Women in Concrete Poetry* emulate the poets included in my anthology, while others move into performative, diagrammatic and conceptual modes that veer away from the aesthetic premises I have chosen to pursue.

## A Revisionary Anthology

Three concrete poets – Augusto de Campos, Ian Hamilton Finlay
and Gerhard Rühm – carved out definitions of concrete poetry
and wrote about its sources and influences, as we have seen. Of
the three, Augusto has produced concrete poetry during his entire
career and continues to do so to the present day. His poetry varies
widely, from the early *Poetamenos* to *Popcretos* (collaged words and
images), to *Equivocabulos* (play with letters), to the collection *Caixa
Preta* (Black Box). Since around 2000, he has added digital anima-
tion, often with sound, and live performance. Finlay was a prolific
and brilliant writer of concrete poetry during the 1960s. In 1966
he moved to the Pentland Hills in southern Scotland and began
work on his garden, first called Stonypath, then Little Sparta. It
became the venue both for concrete poems rendered as sculpture
and for proverbs, quotations and translations often drawn from the
neo-classical world. Rühm has composed cabaret songs through-
out his career. He wrote most of his sound and concrete poetry
during the 1950s, classifying it with precise names such as 'phonetic
poems', 'typewriter ideograms' and 'constellations'. Concurrently,
and into the 1960s, he produced concrete poems he called 'typo-
collages' and, subsequently, multimedia work with spoken word.

These poets epitomize the defining role, for concrete poetry, of
countries existing on the periphery of the cultures dominant during
the Second World War. When the revival of the avant-garde (outlined
by Augusto and Rühm) came after the war, it occurred neither in
Paris nor in the other war capitals – Berlin, London, Rome, Moscow
– but on the periphery: in Sweden (Fahlström), Switzerland (Eugen
Gomringer), Austria (Ernst Jandl, Gerhard Rühm), Scotland (Finlay),
Brazil (Augusto, Haroldo, Pignatari), Japan (Kitasono Katue, Seiichi
Niikuni).[59] From three of these countries, I have singled out three
poets whose work transformed the genre, each in distinctive ways.
Their oeuvres are much larger and more varied than those of lesser
figures of the concrete poetry movement. Indeed, they made concrete
poetry both a fascinating and a difficult genre and furnish us with a
basis for further exploration.

One observes from the above that concrete poetry took
place in nations. Poets set forth manifestos and essays articulating

their theories of concrete poetry, even as some also sought a new internationalism that would make their poetry accessible across linguistic boundaries. Nationalist groups of poets assumed names, such as Noigandres (Brazil), Wiener Gruppe (Austria) and 'plastic poetry' (Japan), and founded new journals from their countries of origin (*Material* – Swiss; *Poor.Old.Tired.Horse.* – Scottish; *Futura* – German; *vou* – Japanese), while utilizing their journals to publish poetry from around the world.

Taking my cue from this distinctively nationalist and internationalist impulse, I have organized this anthology by country. Whereas alphabetical or chronological organization yields an abrupt and even jarring juxtaposition of poets who often have no relationship to one another (Ian Hamilton Finlay followed by Larry Freifeld, Franz Mon by Edwin Morgan), organization by country makes it possible to compare and contextualize and to appreciate national and transnational styles. For example, readers can both assess the output of individual countries (few may realize that Austria and Japan were so productive) and draw comparisons and contrasts between, say, the concrete poetry of Brazil and Austria. Readers can appreciate Dieter Roth's prodigious output and place his concrete poetry within the context of his Swiss colleagues. For each country, I have organized poets alphabetically and, where I include multiple poems by one figure, chronologically.

Within this mapping, how then to represent the different countries? From a wealth of poets of many nations, I have selected forty concrete poets – in addition to Augusto, Finlay and Rühm – whose work has helped define the movement in significant and exceptional ways. Often the poems in question were produced in underrepresented countries. One example is Austria, where the Wiener Gruppe emerged in the early 1950s, shortly after the Brazilian Noigandres. A circle that demonstrated remarkable talent and originality in its treatment of poetic language, the Wiener Gruppe has long been appreciated in Austria but is overlooked outside, no doubt because German is no longer widely known. The Viennese poets worked in black typography on white paper, rather than in colour, and achieved density of meaning with a spare vocabulary. Sound plays a crucial role in their choice of language. If Rühm was the leader, Friedrich Achleitner and Konrad Bayer were two vital members. Their poetry uses phonic similarity to conceal semantic difference and elicits humour through frequent repetition of homophones. Both poets seek to accentuate the contrast between what we read on the page and what we hear aloud.

Ernst Jandl, shunned by the Wiener Gruppe for writing what they deemed to be traditional poetry, was the only fluent English speaker among the Viennese. Jandl focused principally on sound by maximizing the number of short words and phonemes a single long word can yield and by highlighting words connected by sound, but divergent in meaning. His minimalist and playful approach sometimes consists of permutations of a string of simple words that offer several possible readings. Another Austrian, Heinz Gappmayr, was an artist-theoretician working with the connections between the visual and linguistic production of meaning. The Gappmayr poems included in this anthology experiment with the legibility of phonemes and repeated words.

Japanese concrete poetry is likewise seminal and has been neglected in the West owing largely to the challenges of mastering the language. The poets Kitasono Katue and Seiichi Niikuni surely, as John Solt argued years ago in his definitive study of Kitasono, deserve to be in this anthology. Solt explains how the Brazilians, focused as they were on the concrete poem as 'ideogram', regarded the thousands of ideograms in the Japanese language as a model for reshaping the Western alphabet. Haroldo de Campos studied Japanese and came to credit concrete poetry with 'having enacted a cross-fertilization of East and West'. Indeed, his identification of the phenomenon in which avant-garde poets – both in the East and in the West – sought to disclose the 'universals of poetics' points to the breaking down of linguistic barriers so emphasized by Rühm, Augusto and Jandl in their discussions of concrete poetry. To take this further, and following Solt's argument, the erosion of such barriers moved Japanese concrete poetry from the periphery to the centre, thus challenging the hegemonic position enjoyed internationally by the French and English languages.[60]

The concrete poems by Kitasono and Niikuni that I have chosen demonstrate a succinct language in which one or two ideographs play both a pictorial and a poetic role (as in the use of the radical for 'water' as part of the ideograph for 'ocean', or the addition of three dots to the character for 'river' to signify the character for 'sand-bank').[61] The subtle shifts in meaning that result from these delicate changes to the Japanese characters suggest the wealth of visual and semantic nuances offered by a language of ideographs. Repetition of ideographs, moreover, can create both visual and sonic impressions that equate form and content. The versatility of Japanese characters enables the poet to elicit different meanings depending on the character's physical placement in the poem. Because Japanese is so difficult, one needs an expert in order to analyse the poetry.

Just as my emphasis on concrete poetry in Austria and Japan reveals two important traditions little known to the Anglophone world, so this anthology would be incomplete without the poets generally held to be its founders. Eugen Gomringer is considered the pre-eminent among these. His invention of the 'constellation' can be traced through his spatial poem that evokes wind blowing in different directions, his poem suggesting a bouncing ping pong ball, and perhaps his most famous constellation, which conveys silence through language and its absence. These early works are well-deserved classics. Having 'invented' the field during a few pivotal years, Gomringer then turned his attention to professorships at art academies, work as a design and advertising consultant, and the collecting of concrete art and poetry. The French poet Henri Chopin wrote sound poems revolving around repetitions and permutations of individual words, sometimes in the form of onomatopoeia. Chopin intended these poems to be spoken aloud or performed by a virtuoso recitant with often amusing and breathtaking results. Sonic effects generally supersede the visual in his poetic work.

The Swiss poet Dieter Roth, famous for his artists' books, sculptures and works made of everyday materials, focused his concrete poetry on typography as it transforms the look of letters. Rather than utilizing actual words, as did the Wiener Gruppe, Roth played with chains of vowels, consonants and their combinations, as well as with permutations of repeating, non-semantic syllables. He was a chief contributor to the avant-garde magazine *Material* (1958–9), which treated typography as found object, yet his work remains somewhat peripheral to the larger concrete movement.

This anthology also contains selections from poets whose work has unique appeal. For instance, the British Bob Cobbing, principally a sound poet, developed a fascinating and somewhat abstract handwriting for letters of the alphabet. With titles like *Three Poems for Voice and Movement*, Cobbing intended this and other visual texts to be scores for performance. The Scottish Edwin Morgan built a reputation as both a concrete poet and a translator. Immensely gifted in foreign languages, he taught himself Russian and translated Russian *zaum* poetry into Scots. My selections of Morgan illustrate both his fondness for absurd humour and his Russian proclivity. He coined the term 'typestract' ('typewriter' and 'abstract'), moreover, to describe concrete poems produced by Dom Sylvester Houédard on his Olivetti 22 typewriter. Houédard also figures in this anthology, as does the Canadian bpNichol, who linked concrete poetry to such u.s. movements as Black Mountain.

Of special appeal as well are John Cage's *Lecture on Nothing*, typewritten and punctuated to reflect the rubato of speech and tightly structured in units of four, and Carl Andre's 'Elbowelbowelbow' and 'Ititit' from *One Hundred Sonnets*, which follow an impersonal grid form and a thematic organization. Neither Cage nor Andre are typically thought of as concrete poets, yet Cage certainly explored the 'verbivocovisual', while Andre discloses unexpected words through repetition, much as Finlay does in poems such as 'Homage to Malevich'.

An American concrete poet less known than Cage and Andre, but well worth highlighting, is Emmett Williams. Close friends with Dieter Roth, Williams played a leading role in the publication of *Material*, a magazine founded by the Romanian-born Swiss poet Daniel Spoerri and the German Claus Bremer. For the first issue, Spoerri assembled each of the printed pages at random, orienting the unnumbered pages without regard to front, back, top or bottom.[62] Spoerri's and Bremer's contributions to this issue, for which the theme was concrete poetry, make use of invented phonetic spellings (Spoerri's 'Das Rezel Kroiz Wort' (The Puzzle Cross Word)) and mirror versions of vowel and consonant patterns (Bremer's 'Lichtfänge baden Sonne'). Williams took on the production of the entire third issue of *Material* (the last published), which he entitled *Konkretionen* (Concretions). This title invoked the unlimited possibilities of the typewriter to create surprising patterns based on the letters of the alphabet. Williams's artist's book *Sweethearts*, which consists entirely of permutations of the title word, verges at times on abstraction.

Several German concrete poets deserve inclusion. Mathias Goeritz (German-Mexican), principally a sculptor and painter, created a series of sculptures made of gold-plated steel that he called *Mensajes* (Messages). The title *Die Goldene Botschaft* (The Golden Message) was invented by Goritz and utilized by the German poet and typographer Hansjörg Mayer when he published Goeritz's minimalist, non-verbal concrete poems in his series of poetry broadsides, *Futura*. The concrete poetry theorist Max Bense saw his poetry printed in Mayer's broadsides as well. Bense shaped his permutating words (three- and four-letters, including 'rio', in different languages) in the form of a mountain, an allusion to Rio de Janeiro. Ferdinand Kriwet, a multimedia artist and poet, chose a poster-size, circular format resembling LP records to array his boldface, upper-case and densely typed asyntactic text in a manner that challenges a legible, linear reading. Franz Mon captures the enticing, abstract forms of letters and numbers by showing them whole or broken, black or white. Among these German poets we see a striking visual range, with less emphasis on the sonic dimension. The Belgian Paul De Vree, however, mixes German, English and Flemish and relies on the 'verbivocovisual', rather than the visualverbal, to bring sound to life.

Haroldo de Campos, one of the great poets of Brazil and, as noted earlier, a major theorist and translator, wrote concrete poetry proper for only a brief period of his life. But those poems he did produce are remarkable. Haroldo tended to work with a small palette of words, which often share near rhymes and internal rhymes. Organization is spatial, rather than by syntax. His *Fala prata* (Silver Speech), for example, utilizes pairs of words that return in new combinations. All end in 'a' with the exception of 'ouro' (gold), the decisive word that shifts from a pairing with silence to a pairing with speech. Haroldo's friend and fellow Noigandres poet Décio Pignatari is best known for his *Beba coca cola* (Drink Coca Cola), an anti-advertisement – more challenging than it first appears – which
explores phonic relationships that produce different and unpredictable

meanings (as in 'beba', followed in the next line by 'babe' – to drool).

Several fellow Brazilians also produced distinctive concrete poetry, and this anthology includes one example of each. Ronaldo Azeredo creates a grid populated with one word, 'velocidade', which takes form gradually through repeated vvvs. Edgard Braga calls attention to the ambiguity of the Portuguese word for firefly (*lume vaga* or *vaga lume*) and utilizes repetition to call out the rhyming 'um' and 'lume'. José Lino Grünewald narrows his poem to two words, 'solo sombra', with an additional two developing out of the sound of 'solo'. Fereira Gullar chooses five nouns to create a seascape in the shape of a rising tide. Pedro Xisto devises permutations of the word 'aboio', a Brazilian cattle-herding song. The Argentinian poet Edgardo Antonio Vigo produces handmade works that he called *cosas*, or 'things'.

Lastly, as a Postlude, I have included a few contemporary poets who represent the varied legacies of the concrete movement. Such choice is inevitably arbitrary: there are so many fine post-concrete poets who merit consideration.[63] My choices therefore represent different facets. Derek Beaulieu's work explodes the semantic: he writes through various texts, creating dense 'lettrist' surfaces and pursuing a sonic dimension. Susan Howe combines Ian Hamilton Finlay's semantic layering and graphic presence of the text with the

Emmett Williams, 1992.

Susan Howe, 2017.

appropriation of textual passages, which she then cuts, collages and partially erases so as to produce a new visionary poetics.[64] Cia Rinne's poetry is reminiscent of the Austrians in its intensive play with puns and sonic affinities, including words in multiple languages, and in its interest in sustaining a minimalism both in writing and in visual expression. But she is more concerned than her forebears with information theory and digital dissemination.[65]

André Vallias is uniquely positioned between the Brazilian concretists and digital poetics. Representing the next generation after Augusto de Campos, Vallias sees himself both as a poet/designer well versed in literary theory and, like the Noigandres, as a translator, in his particular case of German poetry into Portuguese. Vallias embraces multimedia. His poetry is interactive and incorporates the use of computers. One could accurately say that Vallias continues the 'verbivocovisual' tradition, while transforming poetry into either computer-aided designs or digital media that combine background sound with animated, three-dimensional letters and abstract forms. His use of digital technology to make a new kind of diagrammatic gesture shows us where concrete poetry is heading.

Why, finally, has concrete poetry not yet received its due, especially in the English-speaking world? Perhaps the answer lies in the paradox that concrete poetry, with its reductive word choice and its typographic layout that can superficially resemble advertising, *looks* simple and easy. Audiences at concrete exhibitions or readers who come across these texts in journals, often think concrete poetry is just a game or a craft – rather like Scrabble or finger painting. I hope the texts in this anthology will lay this misconception to rest. The best concrete poems are visually and sonically compelling –

Cia Rinne, Textival, Gothenburg, 2018.

indeed, difficult and complex and hence requiring close and careful reading. The minimalism of many of these poems is deceptive: spare does not mean easy!

In the Latin American countries, Scandinavia and other parts of Europe as well as in East Asia, the importance of concrete poetry has long been widely recognized: there is now a large bibliography on the subject. Augusto de Campos, let's recall, won the Pablo Neruda Prize in Chile and the Janus Pannonius Grand Prize for Poetry in Hungary. But in the Anglophone world, where poetry still tends to be regarded as a vehicle for personal expression and 'big' subjects, even as the visual is equated with painting, and music with familiar genres from song to symphony, and where 'intermedia' generally refers to performance art or installation, concretism has been surprisingly neglected. I hope that this anthology will bring new audiences to what is so clearly a major movement.

# AUGUSTO DE CAMPOS

dias         dias         dias

            **sem**

            **uma**

esperança        **linha**      deum só dia

expoeta expira:       **minh**      **ahcartas**

      sphynx e      **a**      **n ão p artas**

       gypt y g      **mor**      **- E avião voas ?**

                              **- Heli s sim sem ar**

         L EMBRAS  **amemor**     **fim confim sim**

es   DEMIMLYG     **IA e**      **far par avante**

se               **stertor**     **AR**

                **rticula:**     **s e p a r a m a n t e**

ohes        OH SE ME    tele    **NÃO**

se    **- Urge t g b sds vg filhazeredo pt**

segur    sos    se    só    **segúramor**

           LEMBRA E QUANTO

---

*amor* = love; *amemor* = memory; *dias* = days

The *Klangfarbenmelodie* (melody of tone colours) of the modernist Viennese composer Anton Webern provided an important inspiration for Augusto's first collection of concrete poetry. 'Dias dias dias', the sixth and final poem, is animated by the poet's lover, Lygia Azeredo. Augusto abandons conventional syntax and verse and creates a spatial reading of the differently coloured words and letters and their corresponding themes. In red, for instance, arrayed vertically, he creates a 'verbivocovisual' relationship between 'amor' (love), 'amemor' (memory) and 'ɪᴀ' (Lygia).

com  can
som  tem

con  ten  tam
tem  são  bem

    tom  sem
    bem  som

com som = with sound; *cantem* = let's sing; *contem* = let's tell; *tensão* = tension; *tambem* = sounding; *tombem* = let's fall; *sem som* = without sound

The word 'tensão' stands at the midpoint of this poem, articulated in two three-letter syllables. Six pairs of words and morphemes radiate out from it, creating a spatial sound poem that highlights rhyming *m*'s and *n*'s. Under tension, and between opposite poles, the rhyming morphemes move temporally, from sound to silence.

```
sem um numero
   um numero
      numero
         zero
            um
               o
                nu
                 mero
                  numero
                   um numero
                    um sem numero
```

sem = without; *um* = a/one; *o* = the/zero; *nu* = naked; *mero* = mere; *um sem numero* = without number, numberless

This poem's opening phrase provides the source for all subsequent words, including a fourth identical in Portuguese and English – *zero*. Augusto dramatizes the central status of o, Portuguese for *the*, but visually, the number zero, by placing it at the centre of his poem and printing the text to yield two circles (zeros) of white space on either side. He builds his poem back up with sounds that are in fact words: *nu, mero*. His reduced palette and multiple verbal/ visual strategies for expressing 'zero' find a sonic dimension in the recurring 'um', 'num' and 'o'.

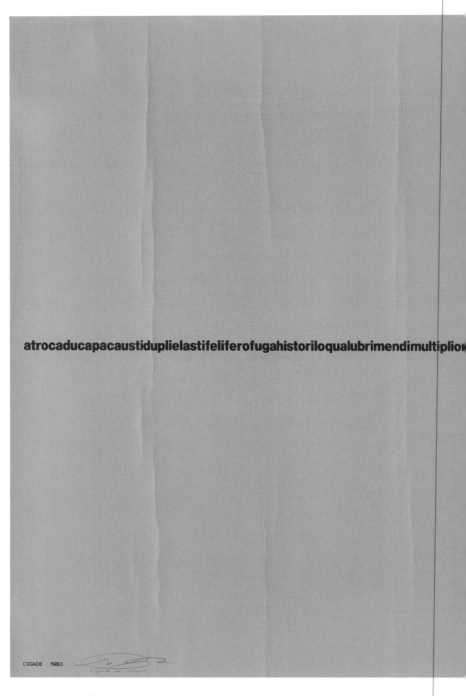

atrocaducapacaustiduplielastifeliferofugahistoriloqualubrimendimultiplio...

CIDADE 1963

This non-syntactical poem is made up of a long, unbroken series of word roots that end in the suffix -*cidade*, -*city*, -*cité* (Portuguese, English and French cognates). Every root and suffix form a real word in all three languages (for example, *atrocidade*, atrocity, *atrocité*). By isolating the roots and organizing them in alphabetical order, Augusto releases semantic control and

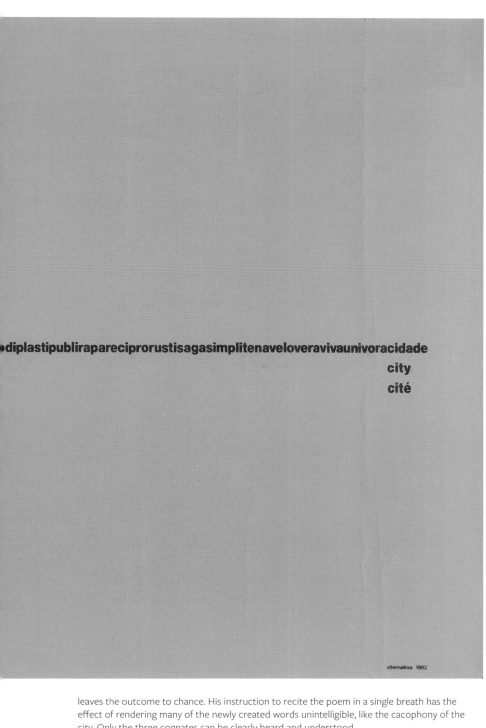

•diplastipublirapareciprorustisagasimplitenaveloveravivaunivoracidade
city
cité

leaves the outcome to chance. His instruction to recite the poem in a single breath has the effect of rendering many of the newly created words unintelligible, like the cacophony of the city. Only the three cognates can be clearly heard and understood.

```
caracol ocar
amas caracol
ocaramas car
acol ocarama
s caracol oca
ramas caraco
l ocaramas ca
racol ocaram
as caracol oc
aramas carac
ol ocaramas c
aracol ocara
mas caracolo
caramas cara
```

*caracol* = snail; *cara* = face; *mascara* = mask; *colocar a mascara* = put on the mask

This poem in the form of a grid allows for multiple readings. In addition to the repeated boldface 'caracol', one can read ongoing statements of 'colocar a mascara'. 'Cara', 'mascara' and 'mascar' are all contained within this set of words. The mask is the shell of the snail that conceals its face. Augusto's metapoem thus masks and unmasks its structure, discovering and describing itself little by little in the process of repeated discourse.

*olho* = eye

This poem belongs to a group that Augusto called *Popcretos*, that is, poems consisting of a collage of magazine clippings from popular culture. In 'Olho por olho', images of human eyes mingle with traffic signs ('danger' at the summit; 'no left turn' and 'one way' on the line below), headlights and a few female mouths. The eyes in each line can be traced to actual movie stars and political figures. By reproducing single eyes, Augusto creates a haunting image that alludes both to the Tower of Babel and to the law of retaliation, 'An eye for an eye, a tooth for a tooth.'

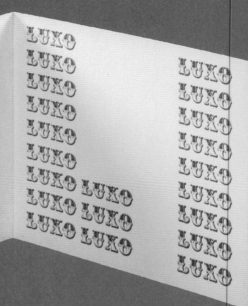

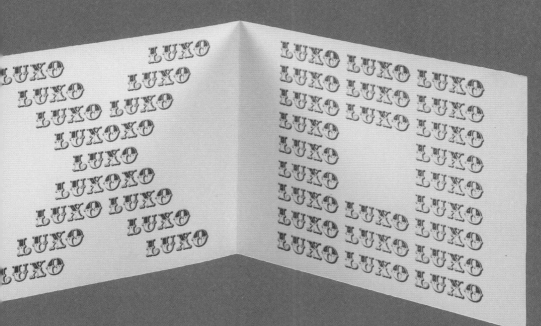

*lixo* = garbage; *luxo* = luxury

Augusto designs repetitions of the word *luxo* (luxury) as building blocks to produce the large letter forms of *lixo* (garbage), a word almost identical in spelling and similar phonically, but opposite in meaning. The kinetic fold-out reveals the word gradually. Augusto appropriated the decorative Baroque typography from magazine advertisements for luxury apartments. The visual effect is satirical and kitsch. Semantically, the constellation of letters brings about the proposition that luxury produces waste.

*linguaviagem* (neologism) = language voyage; *vialinguagem* (neologism) = a way through language; *lingua* = tongue, language; *via* = via; *linguagem* = language; *viagem* = voyage

This 'cubepoem', a format of Augusto's invention, consists of five words generated from the portmanteau term *linguaviagem*. Augusto breaks down the different words into three letters on each face of the cube, outer and inner. The only actual three-letter word is *via*. The poet thus invites the reader to come with him on a voyage through language and to form words by putting the syllables together.

VIVA VAIA (1972)
augusto de campos

*viva* = hurrah; *vaia* = hissing

This emblematic one-word poem – or, more precisely, two words pressed into a one-unit ideogram – was conceived at a concert in São Paulo during Brazil's military dictatorship. The nationalist leftists rebelled against the extravagant performance style of the Brazilian singer Caetano Veloso, who defended himself bravely. The incident inspired the paradoxical title of this poem, in which two words hold opposite meanings, yet share the same letters and a phonological kinship (two syllables, initial *v*, closing *a*). The triangular letters reference the pyramids Augusto had seen on a recent trip to Mexico.

*codigo* = code

At the centre of this poem is the famous palindrome 'god / dog'. Additional readings, which result from dividing 'codigo' in two, yield 'digo' (I say) and 'co-digo', a neologism that suggests a collective statement. The entire poem can function as a representation of the world evoked by the shape of a globe spinning through the ideogram.

In 1968 Augusto met the Spanish-born artist Julio Plaza, who was creating his first 'objetos', non-books consisting of superimposed cardboard pages that projected three-dimensional pop-up forms. Augusto suggested associating these objects with poetic texts, thus conceiving the 'poemobiles', object-poems in which words inscribed on several planes displace themselves when the leaves are opened, making it possible to detect different words. In *Open* (shown here with the leaves fully open), Augusto creates a dialogue between the verbal ('red open half red') and the nonverbal ('blu low yell').

Wherever you may be
On Mars or El Dorado
Open a window to see
The pulsar nearly mute
Embrace of light years
That no sun cheers
And emptied echoes oversee

In this poem, Augusto replaces the vowel e with a star and the vowel o with a circle that evokes the moon. The stars get progressively smaller and more distant, while the moons grow larger and closer. Both contribute to the poem's extraterrestrial theme of a pulsar, an immensely dense star that sends out a pulse. In Portuguese, 'pulsar' also means 'heartbeat' and 'pulsating'. At the end of the poem, star and moon converge on the single word *oco* (empty). With the star in its centre, like a black hole, *oco* can also be read as *eco* (echo). Sonically, Augusto creates an abstract play between *o* and *e*.

*tudo está dito* = everything was said; *nada é parfeito* = nothing is perfect; *tudo está visto* = everything was seen; *eis o imprevisto* = here is the unforeseen; *nada é perdido* = nothing is lost; *tudo é infinito* = everything is infinite

Augusto calls this a 'labyrinth-poem which has the look of a graphic riddle with its paths lacking egress'. He published it as part of *Caixa Preta* (Black Box), a collaboration with the Spanish artist Julio Plaza which brought together reinventions of Augusto's earlier works and do-it-yourself cut-paper sculptures. 'Tudo está dito', one such sculpture, can be folded into a cube. The increased availability of elaborate typefaces in the 1970s clearly inspired this poem.

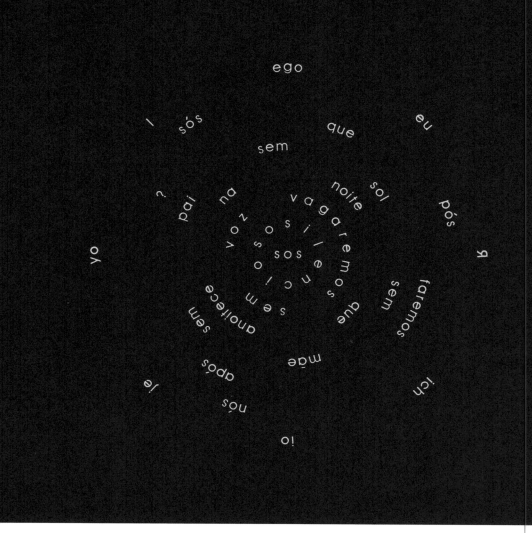

ego eu Я ich io je yo I
nós sós pós
que faremos após?
sem sol sem mãe sem pai
na noite que anoitece
vagaremos sem voz
silencioso sos

ego eu Я ich io je yo I
We alone after
What shall we do after
Without sun, without mother, without father
In the night that becomes night
We shall wander without voice
Silently sos

'sos' began its life as a concrete poem, but by 2000 Augusto had reconstructed this poetic form as a digital animation. Opening with the personal pronoun, 'I', in eight languages, on the outermost circle of text, the poem reads from exterior to interior until it arrives on the acronym 'sos' at the centre. The text contemplates the darkness and the mystery of the afterlife, using multiple languages to suggest that we all confront it together.

*quis* = I wanted; *mudar* = to change; *mudei* = I changed; *tudo* = everything; *agora* = now; *póstudo* = after everything; *extudo* = from everything; *mudo* = I change/mute

In this spare poem, Augusto works principally with two words: *mudar* (to change) and *tudo* (everything). Through variants such as *mudo*, he takes advantage of double meanings. Serving as the poem's final word, *mudo* means both 'I change' and 'mute'. The combination suggests the poet's desire and inability to change. Augusto highlights *mudo* typographically by left-justifying its three variants, just as he aligns the three repetitions of *tudo*.

# GERHARD RÜHM

d d d t
d t
d d a t
d
dat
d
at
td
d d d t
d
td d
aa
a
at d
td
d
td
td a
t t t t d

*da* = there; *Datum* = date; *tat* = (imperfect) to do, (noun) deed, fact

Attempts to create language in this poem do not quite work out. We hear 'dat', which hints at 'Datum', and 'da' emerges from 'dat'. Towards the end of the poem we can hear 'tat', without actually seeing it. Ultimately, the 'tat' does not take place. The poem epitomizes what Rühm calls the 'individual language-sound' ('die einzelnen Sprachlaute') from which words are made.

This phonetic poem of three vowels (*u, ü, i*) is one of the most minimal that Rühm produced. One can read aloud in any direction, with a break caused by the interruption of *i* with *ü* and *u* with *ü*, both taking place at the midpoint of the cross.

```
                            e

                        ä

                    e       ä       e

                e       e       a

            e       e       e       a       a

        e                   e       a       a

    ä           ä               ä       a       a

e                                   ä       a

e                       e       a       ä       a
```

In this sound poem, Rühm arranges three letters (*a*, *ä*, *e*), which sound almost identical, in a broken triangular shape. One can read the vowels in any direction. A perfect isosceles triangle is formed by the group of *e*'s within the upper left of the broken triangle, emphasizing sameness and difference.

```
d
üd
müd
 müd
  müd
   müd
    müd
     müd
      müd
       müd
        müd
         müd
          müd
           müd
            müd
             müd
              müd
               müd
                müd
                 müd
                  müd
                   müd
                    müd
                     müd
                      müd
                       müd
                        m  ü  d
                          m   ü   d
                            m    ü    d
                              m     ü     d
                                m        d       u
                             mu t
```

*müd* = tired; *mut* = courage; *du* = you

Intended to be read aloud, Rühm's typewriter ideogram utilizes repetition to elicit subtle shifts in sound and hence in meaning. Ultimately, 'müd' falls apart as its letters scatter, and 'üd' becomes 'ut' ('mut'), as well as 'du'. The voiced *d* and voiceless *t* produce a subtle distinction between sonically similar words that belong to different parts of speech.

```
dicht h t
d i c h  t
 d   i   c    h     t
 d    i     c     h       t
 d     i      c      h        t
 d      i       c       h         t
 d       i        c        h          t
 d        i         c         h           t
 d         i          c          h            t
 d          i           c           h             t
 d           i            c            h              t
 d            i             c             h               t
 d             i              c              h                t
 d              i               c               h                 t
 d               i                c                h                  t
 d                i                 c                 h                   t
 d                 i                  c                  h                    t
 d                  i                   c                   h                     t
```

*dicht* (adj.) = thick, dense; *dicht* (adv.) = thickly, densely; *Dichte* = (physics) density; *dichten* = to write poetry, to poeticize; *Dichter* = poet; *das Gedicht* = poem; *dich* = you (first person)

Rühm chooses a single word with various meanings. His literal representation clusters the letters of 'dicht' close together at the top (thick) and gradually opens up the spaces in between to produce the opposite (thin). 'Dicht' (the adjective) suggests 'dichten' (the verb 'to poeticize'), 'Dichter' (the noun 'poet') and 'Gedichte' (poetry). Thus Rühm applies a minimalist approach to achieve a maximalist range of implied meanings.

```
schlaf schlaf schlaf schlaf schlaf schlaf schlaf schlaf schlaf schlaf schlaf schlaf schlaf
 schlaf schlaf schlaf schlaf schlaf schlaf schlaf schlaf schlaf schlaf schlaf schlaf
  schlaf schlaf schlaf schlaf schlaf schlaf schlaf schlaf schlaf schlaf
   schlaf schlaf schlaf schlaf schlaf schlaf schlaf schlaf
    schlaf schlaf schlaf schlaf schlaf
     schlaf schlaf schlaf
          falsch
     schlaf schlaf schlaf
    schlaf schlaf schlaf schlaf schlaf
   schlaf schlaf schlaf schlaf schlaf schlaf schlaf schlaf
  schlaf schlaf schlaf schlaf schlaf schlaf schlaf schlaf schlaf schlaf
 schlaf schlaf schlaf schlaf schlaf schlaf schlaf schlaf schlaf schlaf schlaf schlaf
schlaf schlaf schlaf schlaf schlaf schlaf schlaf schlaf schlaf schlaf schlaf schlaf schlaf
```

*Schlaf* = sleep; *falsch* = wrong, false

Rühm's poem is ingenious in its effective use of a palindrome: 'falsch' is the retrograde of 'Schlaf', assuming that the consonant cluster 'sch' always reads from left to right. The single appearance of 'falsch' as a hinge between two textual pyramids raises the question: in addition to the palindrome, what is the relationship between the two words? It lies in Rühm's permutation of the same six letters.

```
                         leer
                         leer
                         leer
                         leer
                         leer
                         leer
                         leer
                         leer
                         leer
                         leer
                         leer
                         leer
                         leer
                         leer
                         leer
                         leer
                         leer
                         leer
                         leer
                         leer
                         leer
                         leer
                         leer
                         leer
                         leer
                         leer
                         leer
                         leer
                         leer
                         leer
                         leer
                         leer
                         leer
                         leer
                         leer
                         leer
lärm lärm lärm lärm lärm lärm lärm lärm    lärm lärm lärm lärm lärm lärm lärm
                         leer
                         leer
                         leer
                         leer
                         leer
                         leer
                         leer
                         leer
                         leer
                         leer
                         leer
                         leer
                         leer
                         leer
                         leer
                         leer
```

*leer* (adj.) = empty, blank, clean; *Lärm* (noun) = noise

The two words comprising this poem are not opposites, but Rühm's setting highlights their contrasting meanings and parts of speech. Reading from left to right, the sound of noise ('Lärm') intrudes on a continuous vertical column which restates 'leer', that is, empty. Rühm empties one slot where the two words intersect and cancel each other out.

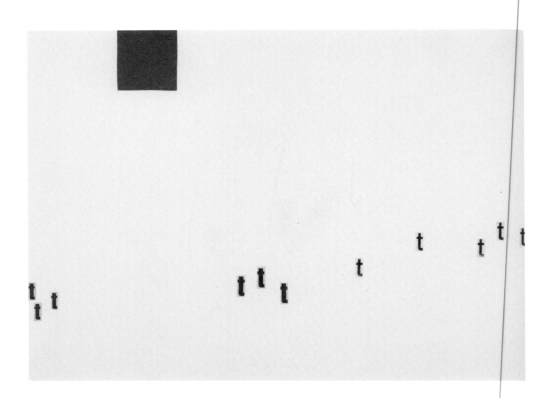

In this 'typo-collage', to use Rühm's term, the poet arranges different versions of a cut-out lowercase *t* in order to encourage successive readings of the voiceless *t* sound. He groups the first three *t*'s close together, expands them into a larger triangle in the middle, and finishes at the far right edge with another triangle formation, although the *t*'s have now lost their heavy, bold look. The moving letters – evocative of marching stick figures – are juxtaposed with a collaged blue-black square above. Rühm thus accentuates both the tension and the common ground between geometric abstraction and mobile 'letter constellations', which 'hover freely in a space that no longer knows the boundaries of language'.

```
wand      wand      wand      wand
    bild      bild      bild
wand      wand      wand      wand
    bild      bild      bild
wand      wand      wand      wand
            wild      wild
                hand
                      wild
        hand      hand
            wild
                      wund
```

Wand = wall; *Bild* = picture; *wild* = wild; *Hand* = hand; *wund* = sore (adj.) (*die Wunde* = the wound)

In this poem, Rühm creates playful repetitions of monosyllabic words which relate to one another semantically, as in a *picture* hangs on a *wall*. Midway, he inserts rhymes ('wild' aligns spatially with 'bild', 'hand' with 'wand'). The surprising final word, 'wund', which is not repeated, seems to come out of nowhere, but could evoke a sore hand. Looked at as a whole, the poem resembles a picture on a wall or a draughtboard pattern.

frau  frau
frAUFrau
     rau  h
glatt
kleid
gleit

       en

*Frau* = woman; *rau* = rough; *glatt* = smooth, straight (hair); *Kleid* = a dress; *gleiten* = glide, slide; *auf* = in/on; *raufen* = to fight

Rühm starts with the whole word – Frau – but then transforms it into 'Lautdichtung' (sound poetry) by highlighting 'AUF'. His splintering of words continues with the syllable 'rau'. Followed by the particle *h*, could Rühm be implying 'rauch' (smoke)? The ensuing monosyllabic word, 'glatt', means the opposite of 'rau', as does 'gleiten', which also contrasts with the implied verb, 'raufen'.

```
fallefallefallefallefallefallefallefallefallefallefallefallefallefallefalle
  fallefallefallefallefallefallefallefallefallefallefallefallefallefalle
    fallefallefallefallefallefallefallefallefallefallefallefalle
      fallefallefallefallefallefallefallefallefallefalle
        fallefallefallefallefallefallefallefalle
          fallefallefallefallefalle
            fallefallefalle
              falle
              all
```

*Falle* = trap/fall (*jemand zu fall bringen* = bring about someone's downfall);
*all* (*alle, aller, alles*) = all

*Falle* is a paragram containing *alle*. Rühm's repetition of 'falle' 64 times sounds as if it will never end, but stops suddenly at the bottom of the inverted pyramid on a word that is both English (personal pronoun) and German (indefinite pronoun). *ll* (fall) is a soft sound, yet an actual fall is hard. In the end, there is only 'all' – a shift from German to English suggesting that the fall is complete.

```
                    g
                   ig
                  tzig
                   i
        sch
        sch        g
        schl
        schl       g
                   ig
        schli
                   t
                   g
        sch  t
        sch  t  g
        schl t
        schl t  g
                  tz
                  tz g
        sch  tz
        schl tz
        sch  tz g
                   ig
                   i
        schli
        schl tz g
        schl tzig
                  itz
                 litz
        schlitz
        schlitz g
        schlitz
                   i
                   g
                  tzig
        schlitzig
```

*Schlitz* = slit, slot; *schlitzäugig* = slit-eyed; *Schlitzohr* = wily devil

Rühm's textual arrangement highlights repeated, harsh-sounding consonants ('sch', 'schl', 'tz', 'g') and inserts the lone vowel *i* only intermittently. Spoken aloud, 'schlitzig' (an invented word) has an unpleasant sound. By breaking it up during the course of the poem, Rühm evokes similar-sounding words with negative connotations, such as *schmutzig* (dirty) and *schlimm* (naughty). If we add new endings, we have 'schlitzäugig' and 'Schlitzohr' – all arising out of 'Schlitz'.

stille
irgendwer sucht mich
stille
        wer sucht mich
stille
            sucht mich
stille
                  ich

*Stille* = quiet, silence; *Irgendwer* = someone; *suchen* = look for; *wer* = who; *mich* = me

This eerie poem begins with the German word for silence. A dialectic ensues between statement and question, always surrounded by 'silence'. First, 'someone is looking for me' (statement), then 'who is looking for me' (question), then a pared-down 'looking for me' (like an echo, could be a statement or a question), ending only with 'ich'. I cannot be found, Rühm seems to say, and so the silence reigns. The spatial division of the text enhances the mystery.

# IAN HAMILTON FINLAY

```
                          a peach
                          an apple
                                        a table
              an eatable
              peach
                    an apple
                                    an eatable
                                    table
                                    apple
                        an apple
                        a peach
```

Finlay's title, 'Rapel', is an invented word referencing the first words of an Irish song in the Glasgow vernacular: 'The ("ra") pale ("pel") moon was shining.' His poem omits syntax and reduces the language to three nouns and an adjective, presented in several permutations, with a use of white space to structure the text. 'Eatable', generated from 'table', elicits humour. Ascribed to 'table', it shifts to nonsense. Finlay also links words through soft rhymes, such as 'apple', 'table' and 'eatable'.

```
lackblockblackb
lockblackblockb
lackblockblackb
lockblackblockb
lackblockblackb
lockblackblockb
lackblockblackb
lockblackblockb
lackblockblackb
lockblackblockb
lackblockblackb
lockblackblockb
lackblockblackb
```

Finlay's concrete poem poses a semiotic enigma that riffs on the abstract enigma of Kazimir Malevich's *Black Square*. Three words – 'lack', 'block', 'black' – emerge from a square of black letters. When isolated, the *b* that forms the right-hand column can be read vertically. When carried over to the left, we begin with black, followed by block, possibly evoking figure and ground. Lock and lack look almost identical but have opposite meanings. Thus Finlay tantalizes with his opposites: stability/instability, presence/absence, black/white.

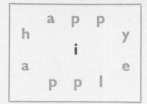

to the painter, Juan Gris                                                                                          i h f

Finlay arrays letters in the elliptical shape of an apple on a rectangular ground, invoking a still-life (hence Juan Gris). The words 'happy apple' audibly share the syllabic break of a double *p*. An *i* in the middle creates a vertical reading, 'pip', suggesting the apple's core of happiness. Semantically, the juxtaposition of 'happy' and 'apple' alludes to the fortuitous fall of Adam and Eve and the beginning of the human race.

*Overleaf*

Finlay defined his standing poems as 'structures of folded paper with printed texts'. This example contains three words or partial words on each side. When the reader activates the poem by turning it around, the structure yields a progression from PEAR to *ppear* to APPEAR, *sappear* to *isappear* to DISAPPEAR, *isappear* to *sappear* to APPEAR, and *ppear* to PEAR. 'Appear' and 'disappear' are opposites, both containing 'pear'.

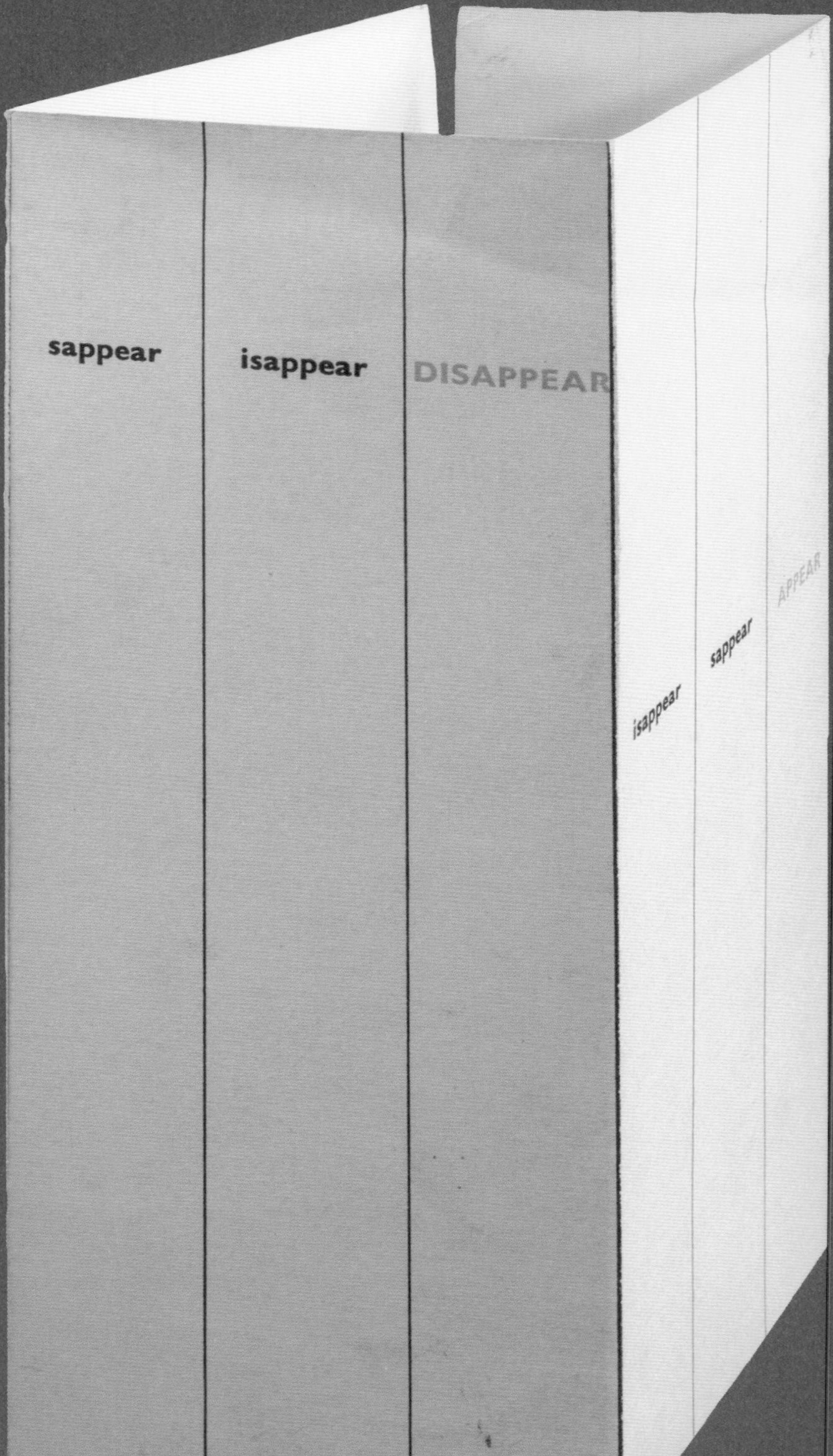
sappear
isappear
DISAPPEAR
isappear
sappear
APPEAR

how blue ?

how sad ?

how small ?

how white ?

how far ?

how blue !

how far !

how sad !

how small !

how white !

first suprematist standing poem
ian hamilton finlay

the wild hawthorn press
printed by the salamander press

This minimalist, seemingly simple concrete poem is challenging to parse. The exclamations in blue on the right do not answer the questions in brown on the left. Moreover, the questions 'how far?' and 'how small?' are not parallel, since the former requires a specific number, while the latter is a relative term. The poem's title refers to the Suprematism of Malevich, whose non-objective paintings were first unveiled in St Petersburg in 1915. Yet while creating a 'model of order' akin to Malevich's 'perfected objects', Finlay's concretism casts an ironic, semiotic spin.

```
paper pear
      paper pear paper
      pear paper pear
            paper pear
```

Gomringer's two-word constellation 'Ping Pong' (1953) served as the inspiration for Finlay's *6 Small Pears*, a group he called 'wee ping/pong variants'. Both an homage and a gentle parody, 'Paper Pear' (one of the six poems) highlights the pun on 'pear' and 'pair', the latter referring to Finlay's rotation between two words: paper and pear. Both share the same letters (anagrams) and first and last consonants ($p$, $r$).

This poem in the shape of a large *S* appears to be a one-word poem until the ongoing repetition of 'star' shifts abruptly in the final line to 'steer', both containing the *st* and *r* consonance. Retrospectively, the layered semantics of 'star/steer' might allude to fishing boat names, as well as to the starlight that guides boats at sea.

In a letter to the poet Emmett Williams (28 November 1966), Finlay wrote of his 'optical' *Acrobats*: 'The idea is, that one first sees an over-all pattern of letters, set in a rectangle, but when one starts to distinguish individual letters, "a", "c", "r" etc., and the eye, by reflex, starts to travel along the word "acrobats", then the pattern changes, and one starts to see the diagonals, going across and down, across and up, etc. Now the whole pattern becomes animated, and what is happening is like a metaphor about the real acrobats.'

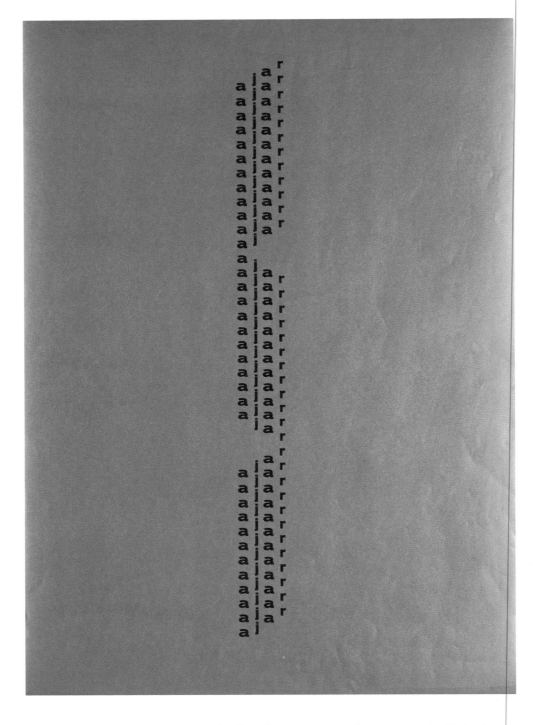

This one-word poem explores the effects of typography on signification. By repeating 'ajar' and placing its letters on shifting diagonals, Finlay encourages a vertical reading (of successive a's, j's and r's), rather than a reading from left to right. His word moves in and out of legibility, like a door opening and closing. 'Ajar' is also 'a jar' (Finlay called it a 'jamjar').

Finlay's arrangement of fishing boat names in a series of concentric circles evokes the shape of a sea poppy, also known as a yellow horned poppy, which grows only on the seashore (hence the blue). All of the names in the poem contain the word 'STAR', resulting in a stylistic mix of designation and description. Boldface highlights 'STAR', without indicating how to group the surrounding words.

```
broken heart
  roken h      t
   oken h       t
    ken h       t
     en h      t
       n h      t
         h      t b
         h      t br
          h      t bro
           h      t brok
            h       t broke
            heart broken
```

In Finlay's poem, the cliché of being 'heartbroken' is redeemed by a new treatment of typographic form. Through the use of spaces, we see the heart emptied of its contents, while 'broken' diminishes one letter at a time. But midway, 'broken' puts itself back together and becomes a whole word, enclosing the empty heart. Finlay seems to ask, 'Is a broken heart the same as being heartbroken?' We consider these words anew, because of their firm and logical structure.

```
                  horizon
                hohorizonon
              hohohorizononon
            hohohohorizonononon
          hohohohohorizononononon
        hohohohohohorizonononononon
      hohohohohohohorizononononononon
    hohohohohohohohorizonononononononon
  hohohohohohohohohorizononononononononon
hohohohohohohohoho       ononononononononon
```

Originally published in a large folio calendar, the title of *The Blue and the Brown Poems* refers to the philosopher Ludwig Wittgenstein's *Blue and Brown Books* (1958). Following Wittgenstein, Finlay's set concentrates on the look and sound of words we think we know and therefore take for granted. 'Ho/Horizon/On' forms a pyramid enclosing new elements of meaning, some in retrograde (*on*, *oh*, *no*, *ho ho*), which overwhelm the visibility of *horizon*.

**ring of waves**
**row of nets**
**string of lights**
**row of fish**
**ring of nets**
**row of roofs**
**string of fish**
**ring of light**

TS, ST, TS: nets / string of lights (st mirrored by ts)

This poem features ten monosyllabic nouns printed in green. Finlay permutates the words preceding the preposition 'of' by making 'row' the second in each pair ('ring row string row ring row'). The pattern shifts in the last line: 'ring' replaces 'row'. The result, 'ring of light', when connected to 'row of roofs', indicates that the boat, with waves behind it, is looking to the shore. Finlay's little poem traces the move from sea (blue) to land (green), its 'ring of light' welcoming the returning sailor.

'Cork net' alludes to the corks that hold up fishing nets pulled by trawlers. 'Ring' suggests the weight that keeps the fishing net down in the water – hence the poem's concentric circles. Reading from the outside in, 'net' becomes a pun for both the fishing 'net' and the 'net price' obtained from selling fish, which are caught both in the net and in the innermost circle of the poem. *cork/net* (five words total) thus epitomizes Finlay's minimalist poetics.

theSEA'S V

The text of this poem appears across three sheets, in an accordion structure that mimics the waves. Finlay's juxtaposition of 'waves' with 'sheaves', the latter distinguished by its silver hue, adds to the layered meanings, which incorporate land and sea. The alliteration on *S* in every word and the echo of the *ea* sound ('sea's' / 'sheaves') reflect Finlay's attention to sound. A secondary reading with a verb – 'the Sea's Waves Heaves' – emerges by omitting the duplicate 'S' at the beginning of 'Sheaves'.

# BRAZIL

```
VVVVVVVVVV
VVVVVVVVVE
VVVVVVVVEL
VVVVVVVELO
VVVVVVELOC
VVVVVELOCI
VVVVELOCID
VVVELOCIDA
VVELOCIDAD
VELOCIDADE
```

*velocidade* = speed

This poem uses the reiteration of vvv as abstract iconography for the word 'velocidade'. The repeated vvv darts down and across the page like an arrow, while diminishing in width with the appearance of each new letter. Ultimately, 'velocidade' appears both vertically on the right side and horizontally on the bottom. Its incorporation of 'cidade' (city) enhances its message of speed.

um = a   vaga-lume = firefly   vaga - flies (verb)   lume = fire (n.)

um
lume      vaga      lume
vaga      um        lume
vaga      lume      um
vaga      vaga      vaga
um        lume      vaga
um        vaga      lume
um

*um* = one; *lume* = fire; *vaga* = flies (verb); *vaga-lume* = firefly

The Scottish concrete poet Edwin Morgan's translation of this poem accentuates Braga's use of only four words. Taking his cue from Braga's glossary definition of *vaga-lume* as firefly, Morgan freely translates 'vaga' as fire and 'lume' as fly. According to Augusto de Campos, Braga 'here gives us his purest concretes'.

<pre>
fala
prata
        cala
        ouro
              cara
              prata
                    coroa
                    ouro
                          fala
                          cala
                    para

        prata                    ouro
        cala                     fala

                                       clara
</pre>

fala / prata = speech / silver; cala / ouro = silence / gold; cara / prata = heads / silver;
coroa / ouro = tails / gold; fala / cala = speech / silence; para = stop; prata / cala = silver / silence;
ouro / fala = gold / speech; clara = clarity

Selecting eight different words and minimal syntax, Haroldo plays with the trite proverb 'Silence is golden,' as well as the classical epithet 'silver-tongued'. A noun and adjective reversal in the final two word-pairs now links silver ('prata') with silence ('cala'), and gold ('ouro') with speech ('fala'). 'Ouro' is the one word that doesn't match any of the others, containing the only *u* and not ending in *a*. Silence may be golden, but in our culture it is gold that speaks.

```
branco        branco        branco        branco

vermelho

estanco       vermelho

              espelho       vermelho

                            estanco    branco
```

*branco* = white; *vermelho* = red; *estanco* = I stop, I end; *espelho* = mirror, I mirror

Haroldo utilizes internal rhymes (*branco / estanco; vermelho / espelho*) and a series of o's that terminate each word and create visual and sonic rhythm. The word 'branco' can represent either the colour white or the absence of everything (blankness). This poem epitomizes the Noigandres group's process of word isolation, in which words assume different meanings depending upon placement and juxtaposition.

mais     mais

menos   mais   e   menos

     mais  ou  menos  sem    mais

            nem  menos  nem   mais

                    nem  menos  menos

*mais* = more; *menos* = less, any less; *e* = and; *ou* = or; *sem* = without; *nem* = neither . . . nor

Consisting of only six words, three of which are conjunctions, this poem relies on repetition and an ideogrammic structure. 'Mais' and 'menos', adjectives or adverbs with opposite meanings, occur six times, 'nem' three times, and 'sem' once. In lieu of syntax, Haroldo inserts spaces of varying widths between words and connects them phonically through the alliteration on *m*. He achieves verbal-visual symmetry by opening with a pair of 'mais' and closing with two 'menos'.

                cristal

                        cristal

                                fome

            cristal

                    cristal

                            fome de forma

                                                    cristal

                                            cristal

                        forma de fome

                                            cristal

                                    cristal

                        forma

*cristal* = crystal; *fome* = hunger; *de* = of; *forma* = form

Haroldo called the technique of the ideogram 'poetic crystallography'. In this poem, he uses language to simulate spatial and symmetrical properties of crystals by mirroring the first four iterations of 'cristal' with the last four. In the middle, he reverses the order of 'fome de forma' ('hunger of form') and aligns 'fome' with 'forma'. Visual placement thus plays a central role in our reading.

```
se
nasce
morre nasce
morre nasce morre
                  renasce remorre renasce
                          remorre renasce
                                  remorre
          re                          re
       desnasce
    desmorre desnasce
desmorre desnasce desmorre
              nascemorrenasce
              morrenasce
              morre
              se
```

se = if; *nasce* = (a human being) is born; *morre* = (a human being) dies; *re*: repetition, rebirth; *desnasce* = (a human being) is unborn; *desmorre* = (a human being) undies

Haroldo structured this poem in four right-angled triangles, bounded at top and bottom by the key thematic word 'se', indicating the role of chance in life and death. The inner links of the triangles are based on 're'. On the far right, the triangle emerges from a repetition of the last letters ('re') of the word 'morre' (to die), followed by a literary rebirth, 'renasce'. The final triangle opens with the theme words 'nascemorrenasce' and closes with 'se'. We have witnessed the flux of life and the poetic epic of its rebirth.

s o l o   s o m b r a

s o l   s o m b r a

s ó   s o m b r a

s o m b r a   s ó

s o m b r a   s o l

s o m b r a   s o l o

*solo* = single; *sombra* = shadow; *sol* = sun; *só* = only; *o* = the

Grünewald was a Brazilian intellectual whose multi-disciplinary expertise included poetry, translation and critical essays. He joined the Noigandres group in 1958. In this concrete poem, the two opening words provide the source (letters) for the three remaining words: 'sol', 'só' and 'o'. 'Sombra' (shadow) is produced by 'sol' (sun), hence a semantic link.

```
mar  azul

mar  azul      marco  azul

mar  azul      marco  azul      barco  azul

mar  azul      marco  azul      barco  azul      arco  azul

mar  azul      marco  azul      barco  azul      arco  azul      ar  azu
```

*mar* = sea; *azul* = blue; *marco* = landmark, sign; *barco* = boat; *arco* = bow, arc; *ar* = air

This poem by Ferreira Gullar, pen name of the Brazilian poet, playwright, essayist and art critic José Ribamar Ferreira, reads vertically. Using 'azul' as a refrain, it consists of two-word columns that replace the first word ('mar'), while decreasing by one line with each repetition. The final line (fifth column) is pared down to 'ar azul' (blue air).

```
              u m
            m o v i
            m e n t o
          c o m p o n d e
        a l é m
                        d a
      n u v e m
            u m
          c a m p o
                d e
          c o m b a t e
            m i r a
          g e m
                    i r a
                        d e
            u m
                  h o r i z o n t e
        p u r o
            n u m
                m o
            m e n t o
        v i v o
```

*um movimento* = a movement; *componde* = composing; *além* = behind; *nuvem* = cloud; *um campo de combate* = a field of battle; *miragem* = mirage; *ira de* = fury of; *horizonte* = the horizon; *puro* = pure; *vivo* = live

Word-for-word translation: a / move / ment / composing / behind / the / cloud / a / field / of / battle / mira / ge / ire / of / a / pure / horizon / at / a / live / mo / ment

Haroldo de Campos describes the verbal-visual dimension of Pignatari's poem as follows: 'Around the axial line of *mm*, words and segments of words constellate themselves, making a kind of verbal *mobile*.' One could add that a reader who accentuates the sound of the letter *m* inserts a phonic component, resulting in a 'verbivocovisual' poem.

beba coca cola = drink coca cola; *babe cola* = drool glue; *beba coca* = drink coca(ine);
*babe cola caco* = drool glue shard; *caco* = shard; *cola* = glue; *cloaca* = cesspool

Pignatari's anti-advertisement reproduces the red and white of the Coca-Cola label.
He develops his poem through transposition: 'beba' (to drink) becomes 'babe' (to
drool) through the switching of the two syllables; cola, printed independently of coca,
is Portuguese for 'glue'. 'Caco', a permutation of 'coca', means shard. By left-justifying
'beba' and 'babe', Pignatari relates them phonically despite their difference in meaning.
Repeated sounds and jaunty colour belie the poem's semantic range and unpleasant
connotations.

```
ra terra ter
rat erra ter
rate rra ter
rater ra ter
raterr a ter
raterra terr
araterra ter
raraterra te
rraraterra t
erraraterra
terraraterra
```

*terra* = earth; *ter* = to have; *erra* = to err; *ara* = to plough; *rara* = rare; *raraterra* = rare earth; *erraraterra* = to be mistaken about / the earth; *terraraterra* = earth ploughs earth; *terra-terra* = plain (simple) things (idiomatic expression)

Haroldo de Campos emphasizes that this poem is ideogrammic; its content is also its structure. Beginning with the syllable *ra*, which immediately forms 'terra' and goes on to generate the word 'erra' (err), Pignatari creates spatial movement in the shape of triangles – one, from 'terra' to *a* (in the middle), a second, from 'terr' to *t*. The large white gap bisecting the poem suggests furrows in the cultivated land. The poem's acoustic level, conveyed entirely through permutations of the source word 'terra', contributes to its content-structure.

Interested in mass media, the Argentine artist Vigo maintained an intimate human touch, producing handmade works that he bluntly called *cosas*, or 'things'. This poem aligns the '4' and the 'W' against the backdrop of a grid and alludes to molecular forms through connected circles.

aboio
oaboi
ioabo
oioab
boioa
aboio
oaboi
ioabo
oioab
boioa
aboio
oaboi
ioabo
oioab
boioa
aboio

The letters comprising the word 'Aboio', a sorrowful, wordless Brazilian cattle-herding song ('boi' is the Portuguese word for ox), cascade across the page, presenting four different non-semantic permutations that each begin with the final letter of the previous one. In 1965 Ian Hamilton Finlay provided the following poignant description: 'The simple permutation of the letters creates the vast space of the plains, and the echoes of the cowboy's cry.'

# AUSTRIA

fastfastfastfastfastfastfastfastfastfastfastfastfastfastfest

*fast* (adv.) = almost, nearly; *fest* (adj.) = solid, firm, tight; *fest* (adv.) = tightly; *das Fest* = celebration, party; *fasten* = to fast; *Fastentag* = day of fasting

Applying Gomringer's principle of the constellation, Achleitner chooses two one-syllable words that sound nearly identical, but have opposite meanings. 'Fast' derives from the German 'fasten' (to fast), while a 'Fest' is a celebration. A fast thus turns into a fest. 'Fast' can also be read as an adverb which, after fourteen repetitions, becomes the adjective 'fest'. In each interpretation, phonic similarity conceals semantic difference and variations in parts of speech.

ruh
und
ruh
und
ruh
und
ruh
und ruh und ruh und ruh und
ruh
und
ruh
und
ruh
und
ruh

*Ruhe* = rest, peace; *Unruhe* = restlessness, uneasiness

In this comical poem, Achleitner calls out for 'rest' by repeating the word 'ruh' numerous times. Yet his alternation of 'ruh' with 'und' results in a new word, 'unruh', noticeable especially when the poem is read aloud. 'Unruh(e)' means the opposite – 'restlessness'. Moreover, the persistent interruptions by 'und' make rest impossible.

# franz war

franz war.
war franz?
franz.
war.
wahr.
war wahr.
wirr.
wir.
franz, wir!
wir, franz.
ihr.
franz war wirr.
war franz irr?
wirrwarr.

*wahr* = true; *war* = was; *wirr* = tousled, confused; *wir* = we; *ihr* = her; *irr* = insane; *wirrwarr* = chaos, clamour

This poem's entire focus on one-syllable words ending in *r*, with the exception of 'Franz', emphasizes homophones (war/wahr, wirr/wir, ihr/irr) Humour stems from accumulated repetition and seemingly random punctuation that contribute nothing to illuminating who Franz is (aside from being crazy) and why he is the subject of the poem. In a poem limited to seven words, the homophones and repetition can drive one mad. Homophones are disguised, however, when the poem is read aloud.

*Quadrat* = square

Gappmayr is among the artist-theoreticians whose texts and artworks have focused since the 1960s on the connections between the visual and linguistic production of meaning. His visual work here comprises black or white letters (or sometimes merely ink stains) peering from within or from the perimeters of a black square, yet impossible to read or pronounce. The square itself can only be a reference to Malevich's *Black Square* of 1915, humorously made mysterious by illegible letters.

s i n d s i n d s i n d s i n d
s i n d s i n d s i n d s i n d
s i n d s i n d s i n d s i n d s i n
s i n d s i n d s i n d s i n d s i n d
s i n d s i n s i n d s i n d s i n d
s i n d s i n d s i n d s i n d
s i n d s i n d s i n d

s i n d n d s i n d i n d
s i n d s i n d s i d
s i n d s i n d
s i n d

*sind* = are (we and they)

Gappmayr chooses one word, 'sind', and deploys it on the page so that the first and last letters merge and the word loses its integrity. In addition to 'sind', we read 'sin', 'in', 'ind', 'dnd', all appearing as Gappmayr avoids a linear arrangement and creates a lively movement of letters not only up and down, but dispersed in space or pressing against one another.

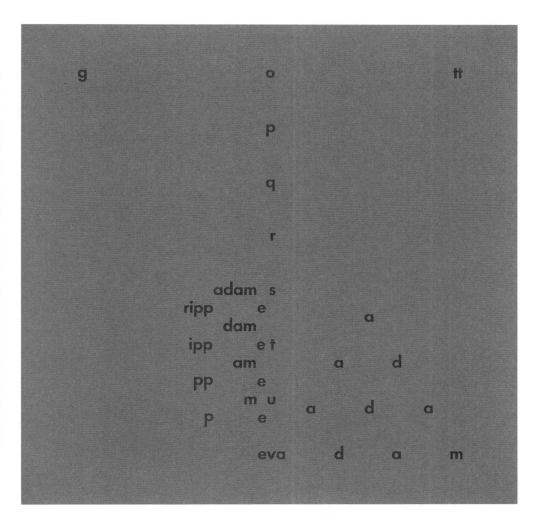

*Erschaffung* = creation; *Gott* = God; *rippe* = rib; *Adam* = Adam; *Eva* = Eve

'Gott' opens this four-word concrete poem, which unveils the alphabet consecutively, from *o* to *p*, *q* and finally to *v*, the middle letter of 'eva'. The alphabet relates to Adam (Aleph), progenitor of mankind and God's first creation. Appearing at midpoint, 'adam' alternates with 'rippe', each breaking down gradually into single letters. The poem thus enacts the biblical story of God's creation of Eve out of Adam's rib. At the end, Adam makes a final appearance through a witty triangle of letters on the right side built from the *a* of 'eva'. Man is thus joined to woman.

ebbeebbeebbeebbeebbeflut
ebbeebbeebbeebbeebbeebbe
ebbeebbeebbeebbeebbeflut
ebbeebbeebbeebbefluuuuut
ebbeebbeebbefluuuuuuuuut
ebbeebbefluuuuuuuuuuuuuut
ebbefluuuuuuuuuuuuuuuuuut
fluuuuuuuuuuuuuuuuuuuuuut
ebbefluuuuuuuuuuuuuuuuuut

In this two-word sound poem, Jandl renders 'ebbe' (low tide) visually abstract through its succession of two *b*'s and two *e*'s and its lack of spacing between repetitions. 'Flut' (high tide) retains its integrity, but with a gradual expansion of the *u* vowel into an implied higher register. Both sonically and visually, Jandl has arranged the proportions so that we experience the ocean's shift from ebbing to rising.

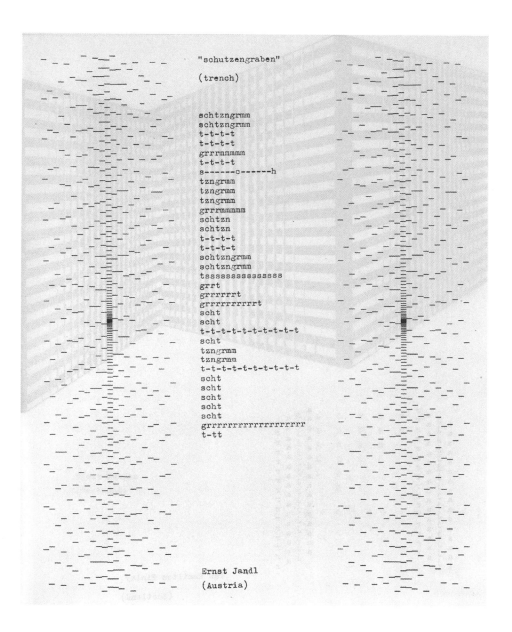

```
                           "schutzengraben"

                           (trench)


                           schtzngrmm
                           schtzngrmm
                           t-t-t-t
                           t-t-t-t
                           grrrmmmmm
                           t-t-t-t
                           s------c------h
                           tzngrmm
                           tzngrmm
                           tzngrmm
                           grrrmmmmm
                           schtzn
                           schtzn
                           t-t-t-t
                           t-t-t-t
                           schtzngrmm
                           schtzngrmm
                           tsssssssssssssss
                           grrt
                           grrrrrrt
                           grrrrrrrrrrt
                           scht
                           scht
                           t-t-t-t-t-t-t-t-t-t
                           scht
                           tzngrmm
                           tzngrmm
                           t-t-t-t-t-t-t-t-t-t
                           scht
                           scht
                           scht
                           scht
                           scht
                           grrrrrrrrrrrrrrrrrrrr
                           t-tt
```

Ernst Jandl

(Austria)

*Schützengraben* = trench

'Schützengraben' is a vivid war poem produced by accentuating the consonants and eliminating the vowels in the German word for trench. This reduced language conceals references to actual words, such as 'gram', in this context a measure of weight of a bomb or shot. Jandl's onomatopoeia provides a sophisticated play on the *parole-in-libertà* (words-in-freedom) of F. T. Marinetti. His repeated consonant clusters ('scht scht scht scht') sound less like guns than like a foul word (*Scheisse* or shit). 'Tzngrmm' connotes telegram, and the repeated 't-t-t' evokes Morse code. The visual dashes in the artwork surrounding the poem, by the Welsh artist Jeffrey Steele, resemble Morse code and are a visual counterpart to what we read and see.

```
wanderung


vom   vom     zum   zum
vom   zum     zum   vom

von   vom   zu  vom

vom   vom     zum   zum

von   zum   zu   zum

vom   zum     zum   vom
vom   vom     zum   zum


und   zuruck
```

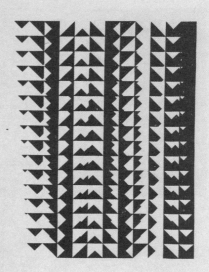

Ernst Jandl

*vom* = *von dem* = from the; *zum* = *zu dem* = to the; *von* = from; *zu* = to; *zurück* = back

Composed of five prepositions, this poem is comical in its circularity and its omission of prepositional objects. Jandl creates a series of permutations through palindrome ('vom zum zum vom'), substitution ('von vom zu vom' 'von zum zu zum') and repetition ('vom vom zum zum'). The final 'und zurück' breaks the regular rhythm while confirming that, indeed, we have gone full circle and will return. The abstract, seemingly three-dimensional drawing by Welsh artist Jeffrey Steele provides a visual counterpart to the poem.

```
st
   und
        en
   und
st
   und
        en
   und
st
   und
        en
   und
st
   und
        en
```

Ernst Jandl

*Stunden* = hours; *und* = and

The playfulness of this small poem arises from the possibility of three different readings. If one focuses on the 'und', one reads as a chain: 'stunden und stunden und . . .'. Separating the word into particles results in 'st' 'und' 'en' 'und' 'st' 'und' 'en' – a sound poem. The full word can be highlighted by reading on the diagonal, up to down followed by down to up, eliminating 'und' as a connector. Welsh artist Jeffrey Steele provided the optical design.

neu

lich
lich
lich
lich

lieb
schreck
frei

neul

ich
ich
ich
ich

liebl
schreckl
freil

neuli

ch
ch
ch
ch

liebli
schreckli
freili

neulich = recently; neu = new; lieb = dear, sweet; lieblich = charming; Schreck = scare;
schrecklich = terrible; frei = free; freilich = quickly

Three prefixes derived from 'neulich' introduce the three parts of this poem, each followed
by all or part of the suffix 'lich' and by three words, or partial words, which shift in meaning if
the suffix is added. Jandl consistently provides four iterations of 'lich' and its variants so as to
link them to 'neu' and to the three words. By utilizing sonic fragments, he creates humour and
conceals the fact that his poem consists entirely of actual words.

# eins

gemeinsamen
gemeinsame
gemeinsam
gemein
mein
ein
einsam
einsame
einsamen
samen
amen
eins

*gemeinsamen* = shared, together; *gemein* = shoddy, vulgar; *mein* = my; *ein* = a; *einsam* = lonely; *Samen* = seed; *amen* = so be it; *eins* = a single one

The word 'gemeinsamen' contains, in addition to 'ein' and 'eins', 'Samen', 'mein' and 'amen'. Stressing 'mein' and 'ein', Jandl moves out towards 'eins' and uncovers a contrast between 'gemeinsamen' (shared) and 'eins' (a single one). In between, he reveals two words which have more distant meanings, but share the 'ein' and 'eins': 'gemein' and 'einsam'. One can only marvel at how many words 'gemeinsamen' yields, connected by sound, but divergent in meaning.

# JAPAN

*Opposite*:

Kitasono combines two ideographs: the first corresponds to the word for 'ocean' (海) and contains on its left side two downward and one upward line representing the radical for water; the second corresponds to the 'apostrophe + s' of English. When repeated as a unit, they create both the visual impression of waves rolling over the ocean surface and the sonic power of the ocean's recurring roar. This equation of form and content gives the poem a concrete dimension.

海の海の海の海の海の海の海の海の海の

海の海の海の海の海の海の海の海の海の海の

海の海の海の海の海の海の海の海の海の海の海の

海の海の海の海の海の海の海の海の海の海の海の海の

海の海の海の海の海の海の海の海の海の海の海の海の海の

海の海の海の海の海の海の海の海の海の海の海の海の海の海の

海の海の海の海の海の海の海の海の海の海の海の海の海の海の海の

海の海の海の海の海の海の海の海の海の海の海の海の海の海の海の海の

海の海の海の海の海の海の海の海の海の海の海の海の海の海の海の海の海の

# MONOTONOUS SPACE

1

white square
within it
white square
within it
black square
within it
black square
within it
yellow square
within it
yellow square
within it
white square
within it
white square

*Monotonous Space* (shown here as part 1 of 4) was Kitasono's only 'official' concrete poem, although he had published 'diagrammatic' poetry in the 1920s and '30s. He wrote it in response to a request from Haroldo de Campos, who had read Kitasono's poems in Japanese and wished to introduce the new Brazilian concrete poetry to Japanese avant-garde poets. Influenced by Josef Albers, Kitasono presents a verbal sequence of repeated images: within a white square is imagined a smaller white square, which dissolves inside the larger one. The same pattern continues with black, yellow and white. The question becomes: for each image, how do we know there are two squares, since they are both the same colour? Kitasono visualizes a phenomenon that is not perceivable.

'I will create poetry through the viewfinder of my camera, out of pieces of paper scraps, boards, glasses, etc. This is the birth of new poetry.' This declaration, from Kitasono's *A Note on Plastic Poetry* (1966), indicates his abandonment of words and the ballpoint pen, in favour of the camera with its ability to capture crumpled newspaper (note the exotic use of Western newsprint), Styrofoam and photographs, such as that of a female eye.

雨

The character for 'rain' at the bottom of Niikuni's poem (雨) is a cluster composed of four dots suggesting raindrops and two horizontal and three vertical lines that convey an element of shelter. Repetitions of four dots in the form of a grid are seen 'raining' above the character. Although the dots do not have an independent meaning, when contextualized within this poem, they assume the role of raindrops.

Niikuni uses a diagonal to divide his poem into two triangular parts. On the left, he repeats the character for 'river' – three adjacent lines moving downwards (川) – so as to create the impression of water flowing. On the right he adds three dots to signify the character for 'sandbank' (州), thus pictorially making a river and sandbank from the arrangement of the repeated characters. The repetition of this pared-down language invites the reader both to visualize river and sandbank and to focus on the characters' abstract forms.

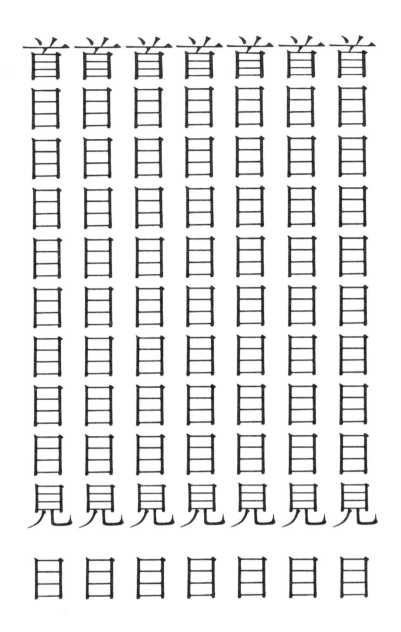

In this intricate poem, Niikuni selects Japanese characters with multiple meanings. The repeated character in the uppermost row (首) means 'head' and 'neck' and also 'top', especially here where it suggests the top of a building. The 目 (eye) parts, occupying eight rows directly below, may be windows seen from the outside or from within. The 'two legs' in the verb 'see' (見) visualize people entering and exiting the building. Between 'see' and the last row is a blank space, possibly a window sill. Throughout, Niikuni plays with the character 目 (eye[s]), appearing in 首 (top, head, neck) and 見 (see).

# UNITED KINGDOM

*Overleaf*:

This folding booklet was produced by poet and scholar Jeremy Adler using a typewriter, stencil, offset and photocopier. Adler plays on the elusive letter 'A'.

Best known as a sound poet, the British Bob Cobbing produced visual texts that were also scores for performance. In the 'e & o' and 'j & f' poems shown here, Cobbing arranges his repeated letters to create the forms of a large *e/o* and *j/f*. Sonically, he followed in the tradition of Kurt Schwitters and Ernst Jandl, but was also interested in 'complex bodily movements and mobile vocal-body sounds in space'.

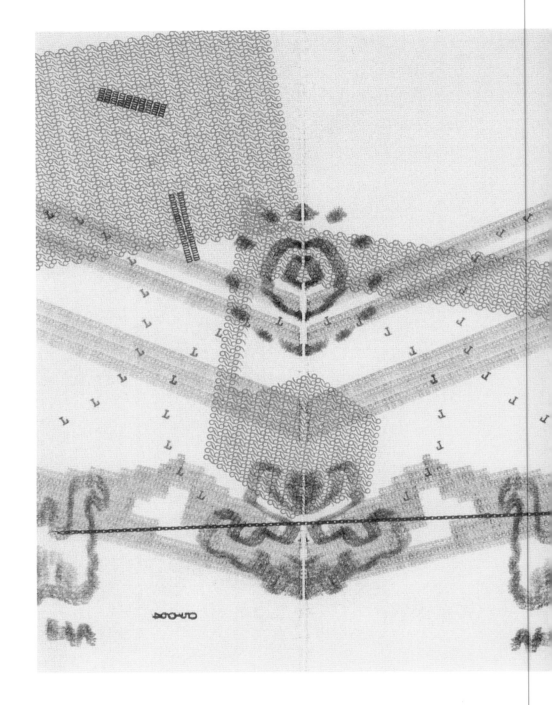

Houédard's Scottish friend Edwin Morgan coined the term 'typestract' ('typewriter' and 'abstract') to describe the concrete poems that Houédard produced on his Olivetti 22 typewriter. The typestracts feature actual words, but other kinds of signs may vie for attention. In *Typestract 051064*, Houédard's repeated 6's (or inverted 9's) in red ink crowd over black letter forms too blurry to decipher.

```
                l
              l o
            l o v e l y
              l o n e l y
            l o v e l y
          l o n e l y
        l o v e l y
      l o n e l y
    l o v e l y
  l o n e l y
      l y
      y
```

**Dom Sylvester Houédard**
**(Guernsey)**

In this spare concrete poem, the change of only one letter alters the meaning of the word: 'lovely' shifts to 'lonely', then back. The reading is both horizontal and vertical. A focus on Houédard's repeated letters, especially *y* and *l*, renders his poem abstract.

# FRENCH PERSIAN CATS HAVING A BALL

```
chat
shah   shah
       chat
            chat   shah   cha   ha
            shah   chat   cha   ha
       shah
       chat
cha
cha


                          ha
                          chat
                          chat
                      chatshahchat
                  chachacha        chachacha
                      shahchatshah
                          shah
                          shah
                          ha


cha
cha
chatcha
      cha
    shahcha
          cha
        chatcha
              cha
          shahcha
                  cha
              chat


                              sh     ch
                                aha
                              ch     sh
```

Edwin  MORGAN

Morgan corresponded with Augusto de Campos and translated some of his poetry into Scottish dialect. Morgan's comical *French Persian Cats* explores repetition by combining the French word for cat (*chat*, pronounced 'sha') with a completely unrelated word, shah, which conveys the 'Persian' reference. He plays these homophones against the English word 'chacha', which looks similar but differs in pronunciation. Intermittently, he inserts 'ha' for humour and virtuosity.

# manifesto

```
r        i      se
              st    an        d
pro            v    e
              st    a                    y
    t    r                               y
r    et  r                               y
  le  ar                  n
        r            e        a        d
    t   r            a           in
        s        tra            in
        v                       i            e
  le  a          e  st
        t        e  st
r    et          e  st
pro     t        e  st
ro      a                r
p               r        e  s                        s
p               ri       s                            e
pr              i                 n                   t
    e                            di                  t
             s             a                 y
proletari               an  s            in
    e            v    e     r                 y
    l                   an             d
        a                 r                      e
  o                       n                      e
proletarii vse stran soediny tes
```

Morgan takes the famous rallying cry from Marx and Engel's *Communist Manifesto* (1848), 'Proletarii vsekh stran soedinytes!' ('Workers of the world, unite!'), and breaks down each word into single letters, clusters or syllables arranged spatially on the page. As such, they can be read aloud in any given order for their sonic quality. Words can be deciphered only with reference to the fully written slogan at the bottom of the page.

# SWITZERLAND

**ciudad**


**avenidas**

**avenidas y flores**


**flores**

**flores y mujeres**


**avenidas**

**avenidas y mujeres**


**avenidas y flores y mujeres y**

**un admirador**

---

ciudad = city; *avenidas* = streets; *flores* = flowers; *mujeres* = women; *admirador* = admirer

*avenidas*, the first example of Gomringer's constellations and written in his native Spanish, repeats the three nouns 'avenues', 'flowers' and 'women', with six repetitions of the conjunction 'and' ('y'), in the following pattern: a, a + b; b, b + c; a, a + c; a + b + c +. We thus move from empty avenues to avenues, flowers and women – all surveyed by *un admirador*, who is the poet.

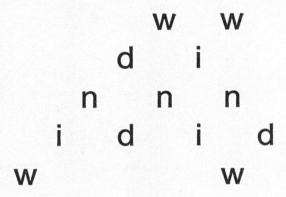

*wind* exemplifies Gomringer's invention of a poem consisting of only one word. Arranged spatially rather than linearly, 'wind' repeats itself in four directions, including three inversions ('wind' read backwards). Gomringer's typography playfully captures the capricious blowing of the wind. His insertion of white space both between the letters and around the poem highlights the poem's abstract quality as an object 'to be both seen and used'.

ping pong
    ping pong ping
    pong ping pong
        ping pong

Repetition highlights the sonic play of 'Ping Pong'. We hear the percussive, alliterative *p*'s and alternating *i*'s and *o*'s, coupled with the repeated final alliterative *ng*'s. Focused on both forward and backward readings, Gomringer shifts from the symmetry of two to the asymmetry of three by adding 'ping' to the end of one line and 'pong' to the beginning of the next. Each instance briefly complicates the clarity of 'ping pong'.

silencio silencio silencio
silencio silencio silencio
silencio          silencio
silencio silencio silencio
silencio silencio silencio

Gomringer made three versions of this poem: Spanish, German and English. While the German was the original, the second, 'silencio', may be the most sonically effective, because of its iambic meter. Gomringer plays off the paradox that we are reading / speaking a word that means silence. In the empty space in the middle of the poem, ground become figure. The grid structure activates a horizontal and vertical reading, as we perceive both the whole and its parts.

```
                                          o
                                          bo
                                          blow
                                          blow blow
                                          blow blow blow
                                          blow blow
                                          blow
                                          bo
          o                               o
          go                              so
          grow                           show
          grow grow              show show
          grow grow grow o show show show
          grow grow              show show
          grow                           show
          go                              so
          o                               o
          lo
         flow
       flow flow
     flow flow flow
       flow flow
         flow
          lo
          o
```

In this minimalist constellation, the title's circle becomes a negative presence. The two circle halves are outlined by four triangles made of the rhyming container words: *grow, flow, blow, show.* The central line 'grow grow grow' is followed by an *o*, as if to say: how amazing that things grow. The following 'show show show' suggests 'show me/us'. At the apex of each unit appear the four *o*'s. Multi-directional readings reveal small words built from the container words: lo, go, so, bo.

fliegt

       strömt entgegen

fliegt

       breitet sich aus

fliegt

       umhüllt

fliegt

       verdünnt sich

fliegt

       löst sich auf

fliegt

*fliegen* = fly; *strömen* = stream, pour; *entgegen* = towards; *sich ausbreiten* = spread out, open out; *umhüllen* = shroud; *sich verdünnen* = dilute; *sich auflösen* = dissolve itself

Gomringer crafts his poem around verbs in the third-person singular, but without naming the agent. The repeated 'fliegt' (s/he/it flies) acts as a refrain/litany, alternating with verbs about water (streams towards, dilutes) and about taking cover (shrouds). Although this poem experiments less with concision and inversion than Gomringer's other constellations, the structure of two word-columns invites a live reading that pauses in the empty spaces, allowing 'fliegt' to resonate.

mann                                          hund


**frau**


kind                                          vogel


*Mann* = husband; *Frau* = wife; *Kind* = child; *Hund* = dog; *Vogel* = bird

The vocabulary in this 'constellation' aspires to a universal concrete poetry by using simple, mostly one-syllable words, three on the left (suggesting members of a family) and two on the right (animals). The words' parallel placement on facing pages and the large empty spaces between vertical readings isolate the sound of each.

beweglich
weil weglos


weil weglos
leicht


leicht
weil machtlos


weil machtlos
gefährlich


gefährlich
weil beweglich


weil beweglich
weglos


weglos
weil leicht


weil leicht
machtlos


machtlos
weil gefährlich


weil gefährlich
beweglich


*beweglich* = movable, mobile; *weil* = because; *weglos* = pathless; *machtlos* = powerless;
*gefährlich* = dangerous

Gomringer's purpose here is to make a little statement about the word 'weil' (because).
He shows how it produces constant changes in meaning depending on its partner words.
The text's lack of punning, inversion or condensation move it away from concrete poetry.

worte sind schatten
schatten werden worte


worte sind spiele
spiele werden worte


sind schatten worte
werden worte spiele


sind spiele worte
werden worte schatten


sind worte schatten
werden spiele worte


sind worte spiele
werden schatten worte


*Worte* = words; *Schatten* = shadows; *werden* = become; *Spiele* = games

This poem plays on the idea that if you reverse the order of simple words in simple units, the meaning changes. Gomringer departs from concretism by focusing less on multilinearity, reduction, layered meaning and the semantic implications of structured space and more on a very basic level of permutation.

atoretoratorateroterat

```
  r r r         r r r         r r r         r r r         r r r          r r r
    e e             a a         a a             e e         a a              a a
              a a                             a a           e e              o o
a a             e e             o o         o o           o o              e e
o o             o o             e e
```

```
      r   r t t   t r r   r t t   t r r   r t t   t r         r           t
      e a o o a e a e o o e a a o e e o a era otota erar
```

```
      r r t t t r r r t t t t r r r t t t   r
      a o o a         e o o e         o e e o
      e     e         a     a         a     a
```

```
      r         r     r         r     r         r
      r t t t     r t t t     r t t t
      a o o a     e o o e     o e e o
      e     e     a     a     a     a
```

```
      r         r     r         r     r         r
      r t t t     r t t t     r t t t
      o o         o o         e e
      e a a e     a e e a     a o o a
```

```
      r r t r     r r t r     r r t r
        t t         t t         t t
      o o         o o         e e
      e a a e     a e e a     a o o a
```

```
      r r t r     r r t r     r r t r
        t t         t t         t t
      o o         o o         e e
      a a         e e         o o
      e e         a a         a a
      r r         r r         r r
      r t         r t         r t
      t t         t t         t t
      o o         o o         e e
      a a         e e         o o
      e e         a a         a a
        r r         r r         r r
        t   r       t   r       t   r
        t t         t t         t t
      oo           oo           ee
      a a         e e         o o
      ee           aa           aa
      t r r       t r r       t r r
```

```
      t t r       t t r       t t r
      ooa         ooe         eeo

      aee         eaa         oaa
        t r         t r         t r
        t   r       t   r       t   r
```

Using the Icelandic word *bok* (book) from the country in which he was living, Dieter Roth opens with two pages of symmetrical letters *d* and *b*, arranged in star-like groups of four, spinning in space. Each letter group differs and sometimes transforms into *p*'s and *q*'s. Pages in *Bok* belong to sequences. Hence, a subsequent page combines vowels and consonants to create the row 'atoretoratoratereroterat', from which his name (Rot) emerges. Variations of his row show the letters upside down in a grid. 'Rot' is simultaneously German for the primary colour 'red' and, when written and pronounced 'ròt', the Icelandic word for 'evil person' or 'disorder'. On a later page Roth creates permutations of his row ('rrr aa oo ee', 'rrr aa ee oo'), separating and grouping the vowels and the consonants.

t
mo
ama
oto
pop
tat
matot
tamopa
ototatam
omamoma
amatoto
apotop
amato
otatop
tomato
apat
at
omo

m

This is one of the few pages in *Bok* that is self-contained. Roth creates permutations principally on the words 'tomato' and 'potato', yet the *zaum*-like syllables generated by these source words challenge the reader to draw connections. 'mo', 'ama', 'oto', 'pop', 'tat' are sufficiently obscure, while 'otatop' is a direct retrograde, and 'ototatam' reads as 'tomato' when you shuffle the letters and eliminate the extra 't'.

ra    ra    ra    ra    ra    ar    ra    ra    ra    ra    ar    ar    er    ir
ra    ra    ra    ra    ar    ar    ar    ka    ra    ra    ar    ar    ar    er
ra    ra    ra    ar    ar    ar    ak    af    ka    ra    ar    ar    ar    ra
ra    ra    ar    ar    ar    ak    af    ab    af    ka    ar    ar    ra    ra
ra    ar    ar    ar    ak    af    ab    af    ab    af    ak    ra    ra    ra

Roth's contributions to *Material* no. 1 consist of repeated non-semantic syllables, which he permutates by reversing the order of letters and substituting new consonants. The result is unpredictable patterns of sonic wordplay.

t

u    u    u

t        tu

u

t                    u

t        ut    u

t        t

t

```
                    ain

                    für

    in    für    mit    qeqen    aus

                    qeqen

                    in
```

ain = an (to) or ein (a); *für* = for; *in* = in; *mit* = with; *gegen* = against; *aus* = from (or) out of

Roth's phonetic orthography produces an intimate, childlike expression that he cultivated in reaction to the detachment of the abstract and concrete artists and poets. *ain für mit* consists entirely of repeated prepositions, arranged in the form of a cross and legible in any direction.

```
das rezel kroiz wort
rezelt das wort kroiz
wort rezelt das kroiz

das kroiz wort rezel
kroizt das rezel wort
rezel kroizt das wort
```

Spoerri's 'Das Rezel Kroiz Wort' (The Puzzle Cross Word) offers a phonetic orthography akin to Dieter Roth's vernacular writing. Spoerri's 'Ni Ni Selten' (Never Never Seldom) contrasts its title words with 'manchmal', 'oft', 'maistens' and 'imer' – all adverbs that refer differently to time. Principally an editor rather than a poet, Spoerri argued that 'concrete poetry attempts to eliminate the communication of the author's opinion from the work.'

ni
ni
selten
ni
ni
selten
manchmal
ni
ni
selten
ni
ni
selten
manchmal
oft
ni
ni
selten
ni
ni
selten
manchmal
ni
ni
selten
ni
ni
selten
manchmal
oft
maistens

imer

# GERMANY AND FRANCE

ir

o
rio
roi
oro
orior
orion
rionoir
ronronron

ri

A theorist of concrete poetry, Bense analysed the word as a material element of construction. *Tallose Berge*, featuring three- and four-letter permutations, alludes in shape to the mountains of Rio de Janeiro, while combining letters to form new words in multiple languages – 'roi', 'oro', 'orion', 'noir'.

*Lichtfänge* = light trap; *baden* = to bathe; *Sonne* = sun

In this poem, Bremer utilizes mirror versions of 'sonne' and of his lines of vowels ('i ä e a e e!') and consonants ('i chtf ng b hn n d') to create a concrete poem in which only 'sonne' is an actual word. The vowel and consonant lines might be sun rays or a geometric cross.

```
        e
      ei
      ei n
      ei n
      i n t
      n t e
          t ex
      t ext
      ext
      xt   p
      t   pa
        pas
      pas s
      as s i
      s si e
      si er
      i er t
      er t
      r t
      t
```

ein = a; text = text; passiert = happens

Gomringer called Bremer's poems ideograms and a 'genuine enrichment of the constellation'. In this poem, Bremer conceals the legibility of his three words by reducing them to their letter or syllable components, then building up to the actual word, followed by breaking it down into phonemes again. The poem begins with a diagonal of four e's ('ein') and ends with a diagonal of t's ('passiert').

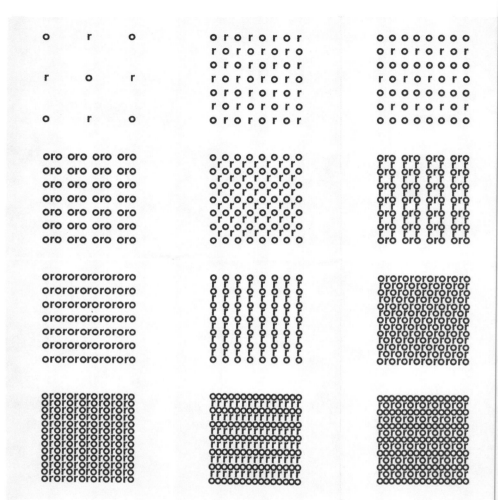

Goeritz called his first concrete poems *Mensajes* (Messages), after a series of sculptures he made of gold-plated steel on wood beginning in c. 1959. His typewritten poems use the *o* and the *r* of the Spanish word 'oro' (gold) to form geometric squares that share the sculpture's reverberating effect. When Hansjörg Mayer discovered Goeritz's concrete poems, he set them in the Futura font and titled them *Die Goldene Botschaft* (The Golden Message). These minimalist poems explore twelve different permutations of 'oro', all in grids that read both vertically and horizontally.

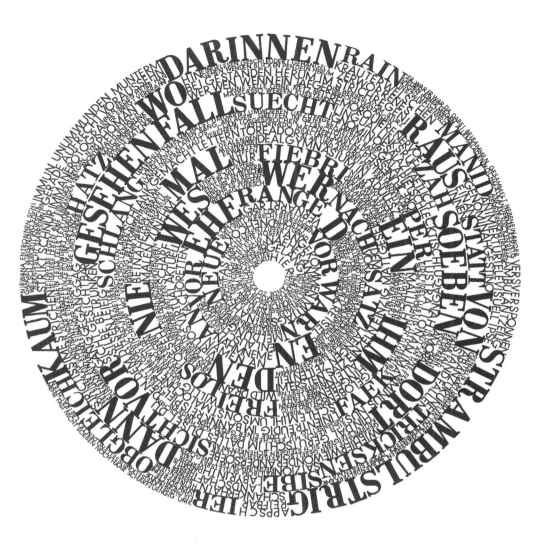

Kriwet's ten *Rundscheiben* (Round Discs), part of his *Sehtexte* (Visual Texts), are poster-size prints that evoke large LP records and work against linear reading. In *Rundscheibe 1*, we read from exterior to interior, from the periphery to the centre of the circle, following the boldface words (some invented, some actual): 'KAUM DARINNEN STRAMBULSTRIG', 'WO RAUS VON DANN', ending with 'EHE D EN'. Between the boldface, Kriwet inserts densely written, asyntactic text. He thus makes visible a new graphic language.

s a u

a u s

u s a

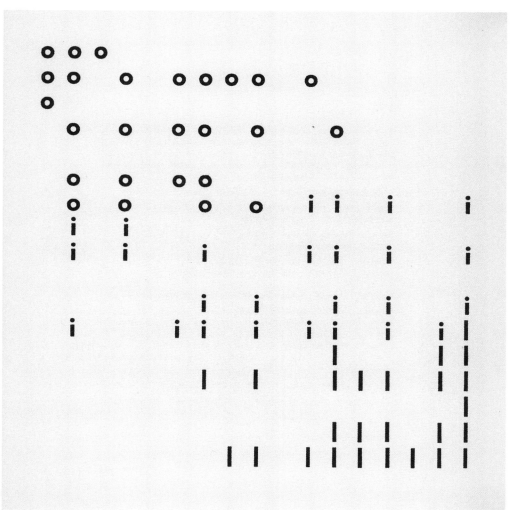

Hansjörg Mayer devised a minimalist approach in order to focus his Futura typeface on a clear, concise use of individual letters of the alphabet. His monoprints, *Typoems 1* and *2*, show the optical structure of letters and the punctuation of text in space. 'sau aus usa' explores permutations of three letters in a grid to arrive at 'aus usa' (translated as 'from the USA').

This black-on-white collage is not legible, but evokes lowercase letters and numbers. The larger forms suggest combinations of *b*, *g* and *e*, as well as the number 9. Smaller forms in the lowest row hint at the vowels *a*, *i* and *u*. Mon's purpose is not to conceal actual letters and numbers, but to highlight their enticing, abstract forms by showing them whole or broken, black or white.

Mon plays with shifting meanings by inserting different vowels between the *t*'s of three-letter words. The verb 'tut' (present tense s/he does) shifts to the adjective 'tot' (dead), followed by the verb 'tat' (past tense s/he did), 'tet' (a common suffix in its 'tät' form), and 'tüt' (related to the idiomatic 'Tüte', which can mean 'Not on your life!').

```
                    vite
                    vite
                    vite
                    vite
             vite vite vite
             vite vite vite
             vite vite vite
             vite vite vite
          vite vite vite vite vite
          vite vite vite vite vite
          vite vite vite vite vite
       vite vite vite vite vite vite vite
       vite vite vite vite vite vite vite
       vite vite vite vite vite vite vite
       vite vite vite vite vite vite vite
    vite vite vite vite vite vite vite vite vite
    vite vite vite vite vite vite vite vite vite
    vite vite vite vite vite vite vite vite vite
    vite vite vite vite vite vite vite vite vite
    vite vite vite vite vite vite vite vite vite
    vite vite vite vite vite vite vite vite vite
 vite vite vite vite vite vite vite vite vite vite
    vite vite vite vite vite vite vite vite
    vite vite vite vite vite vite vite vite
    vite vite vite vite vite vite vite vite
    vite vite vite vite vite vite vite vite
       vite vite vite vite vite vite vite
       vite vite vite vite vite vite vite
       vite vite vite vite vite vite vite
       vite vite vite vite vite vite vite
       vite vite vite vite vite vite vite
          vite vite vite vite vite
          vite vite vite vite vite
          vite vite vite vite vite
          vite vite vite vite vite
          vite vite vite vite vite
             vite vite vite
             vite vite vite
             vite vite vite
             vite vite vite
             vite vite vite
             vite vite vite
             vite vite vite
                    vite
                    vite
                    vite
                    vite
                    vite
                    vite
                    vite

                  vivons
```

poème—graphique
pour un cerf—volant

Chopin was a master of the audio-poem. His interest in 'vocal values in their own right' led him to focus on both sound recording and concrete poetry. After meeting Haroldo de Campos in Paris in 1958, Chopin created *Le dernier roman du monde* (The Last Novel of the World), featuring typeset poems that experimented with repeated letters, syllables and word combinations. *vite* (fast) assumes the shape of a kite tail and enacts its movement through breathless repetitions of a single word.

```
vol  voleauvent  pigeonvole   fairelavole    vo      e       v
vol  voleauvent  pigeonvole   faire avole    vol     e       v
vol  voleauvent  pigeonvole   faire avole    vol     e       v
vol  voleauvent  pigeonvole   fair  vole     vol     e .     v
vol  voleauvent  pigeonvole   faire avole    vol     e       v
vol  voleauvent  .pigeonvole  fairelavole    vol     e       v
vol  voleauvent  pigeonvole   faire avole    vol     e       v
vol  voleauvent  pigeonvole   faire avole    vol     e       v
vol  voleauvent  pigeonvole   fair  vole     vol     e       v
vol  voleauvent  pigeonvole   fair  vole     vol     e       v
vol  voleauvent  pigeonvole   fai   ole      vola    e       v
vol  voleauvent  pigeonvole   fai   ole      vola    e       v
vol  voleauvent  pigeonvole   fai   ole      vola    e       v
vol  voleauvent  pigeonvole   fa    le       vola    e       v
vol  voleauvent  pigeonvole   fa    le       vola    e       v
vol  voleauvent  pigeonvole   fa    le       vola    e       v
vol  voleauvent  pigeonvole   f     e        volä    e       v
vol  voleauvent  pigeonvole   f     e        vola    e       v
vol  voleauvent  p     e                     vola    e       v
vol  voleauvent  p     e      fa    le       vola    e       v
vol  voleauvent  p     e      fa    le       volat   e       v
vol  voleauvent  pi    e      fa    le       volat   e       v
vol  voleauvent  pi    e      fai   ole      volat   e       v
vol  voleauvent  pi    e      fai   ole      volat   e       v
vol      auvent  pig   e      fai   ole      volat   e       v
vol      auvent  pig_  e      fai   ole      volat   e       v
vol      auvent  pig   e      fai   ole      volat   e       v
vol      auvent  pige  e      fair  vole     volat   e       v
vol      auvent  pige  e      fair  vole     volati  e       v
vol      auvent  pige  e      fair  vole     volati  e       v
vol      auvent  pige  e      fair  vole     volati  e       v
vol      auvent  pige  e      faire avóle    volati  e       v
·vol     auvent  pigeo e      faire avole    volati  e       v̇
vol      auvent  pigeo e      faire avole    volati  e       v
vol      auvent  pigeo e      fairelavole    volati  e       v
vol      auvent  pigeo e      fairelavole    volati  e       v
vgl      auvent  pigeo e      fairelavole    volati  e       v
vol      auvent  pigeo e      f     e        volati  e       v
vol      auvent  pigeon e     fa    le       volati  e       v
vol      auvent  pigeon e     fai   ole      volati  e       v
vol      auvent  pigeon e     fair  vole     volati  e       v
vol      auvent  pigeon  e    faire avole    volati  e       v
vol      auvent  pigeon le    fairelavole    volati  e       v
vol      auvent  pigeon le    f              volati  e       v
vol      auvent  pigeon le    fa             volati  e       v
vol      auvent  pigeon ole   fai            volati  e       v
vol      auvent  pigeon ole   fair           volati  e       v
vol      auvent  pigeon ole   faire          volati  e       v
vol      auvent  pigeon ole   fairel         volati  e       v
vol      auvent  pigeon ole   fairela        volati  e       v
vol      auvent  pigeonvole   fairelav       volati  e       v
vol      auvent  pigeonvole   fairelavo      volati  é       v
vol      auvent  pigeonvole   fairelavol     volati  e       v
vol      auvent  pigeonvole   fairelavole    volatile        v
```

In this concrete poem, Chopin develops one word and its sound out of another. 'Vol' (flight) becomes 'voleauvent' (flightwaterwind), 'vol auvent' (flight in the wind, or puff pastry), 'pigeonvole' (pigeonflight), 'fairelavole' (win the vole) and 'volatile' (bird/fowl). Chopin's typewriter poems derive much of their humour from perpetual sonic repetition.

```
                              fff
                              lll
                              aao
                              ccc
                              lll
                              aao
                              ccc
                               l
                               i
                               c
flac flic floc flac flic floc flac flic flic flad floc flic flac floc flic flac
flic flac floc flic flac floc flic flacalf flic flac floc flic flac floc flic
flic flic flic flic flic flic flic flic flic flic flic flic flic flic flic
flac        flic flac floc floc flac floc floc flic flac floc flic flac floc
  flac        floc floc floc floc floc floc floc floc floc floc floc      floc
    flic      flic fluc floc flac flic flac floc flic fluc floc          flic
    flac        flac flic floc flic flac flic fluc flac flic            flic
    flic          flic flac floc flac flic fluc floc flic             flac
    flac          flic..... flac flic fluc flic flac                 flac
    flic          flac..... floc flic fluc flic                     flac
    flac          flic... floc floc flic fl                         flic
    flic          flac. floc flic flic                              flic
    flic            flac flic flic f                                flic
    flic          ...................                               flic
    flac          flic........flic                                  flac
    flac          flic        flic                                  flac
    flac          flic        flic                                  flac
    flac          flic        flic                                  flac
    flic          flic        flic                                  flac
    flac          flic        flic                       flic       flic
    flac          flic        flic                       flic       flic
    flac          flic        flic                       flic       flic
    flic          flic        flic                       flic       flic
    flac          flic        flic                       flic       flic
    flic            flic        flic                        flic flic
                    flic        flic                           flic
                    flic        flic
                    flic        flic
                    flic        flic
                    flic        flic
                    flic        flic
                    flic        flic
                    flic        flic
                    flic        flic
                    flic        flic
        flic flic              flic flic flic
     floc floc floc            floc floc floc floc
     floc floc floc            floc floc floc floc      il patauge
```

The titles of Chopin's concrete poems reveal little about the figures composed of letters on the page. Moreover, aside from the titles, there are often few words to detect. In *Il patauge*, we see only the repeated nonsense syllables *flic flac floc* – onomatopoeic for splashing water. Chopin's design of an instantly recognizable human form pokes fun at the nonreferential or more ambiguous tendencies of concrete poetry.

vertigo gli


S K I b a a n
S K Y l i n e

S T I P          S T I P
                                 stijgt

    BLIinkt
    BLIkt

          BLIK
          BLIK

G L I J b a a n
G L I J v l u c h t

G L E I S

          G L I nstert
          G L I mt
          G L I st
          G L I pt

    de   w i n g
    de   w o n g
    de   w i m p e r

                                 strijkt

s t r e k t   z i c h   d e   h o r i z o n

          H O R I Z O N

          w o e n g

          G R O N D


De Vree arranged to have *Vertigo gli* created electronically on a tape recorder and recited by multiple voices. 'Gli', from the French 'glisser' ('to slide'), references both the ski run and the gliding of an aeroplane ('de wing'), whose motor touches ground ('grond'). Dependent on the 'verbivocovisual', the poem's mix of German, English and Flemish attests to concrete's transnational message.

# UNITED STATES AND CANADA

```
elbowelbowelbowelbowelbowelbow
elbowelbowelbowelbowelbowelbow
elbowelbowelbowelbowelbowelbow
elbowelbowelbowelbowelbowelbow
elbowelbowelbowelbowelbowelbow
elbowelbowelbowelbowelbowelbow
elbowelbowelbowelbowelbowelbow
elbowelbowelbowelbowelbowelbow
elbowelbowelbowelbowelbowelbow
elbowelbowelbowelbowelbowelbow
elbowelbowelbowelbowelbowelbow
elbowelbowelbowelbowelbowelbow
elbowelbowelbowelbowelbowelbow
elbowelbowelbowelbowelbowelbow
```

Andre's *One Hundred Sonnets* is a cycle of poems produced on a mechanical typewriter and hence in grid form. Each is fourteen lines (true to the sonnet) and based on the repetition of one word. The 'cycle' operates through thematic coherence, with one sonnet leading logically to the next. Andre organizes his poems by category (for example, 'Pronouns', 'Body Parts', 'Excretory Functions') and specifies the words he will use within each. 'Elbowbowelbow' comes in the middle of 'Body Parts'. Its repetition yields not only 'bow', but, more visibly and less audibly, 'bowel' ('Excretory Function') and 'ow' (as in 'ouch'). Andre's attention rests on the tactile sense of the words themselves.

```
itititititititititititititititit
itititititititititititititititit
itititititititititititititititit
itititititititititititititititit
itititititititititititititititit
itititititititititititititititit
itititititititititititititititit
itititititititititititititititit
itititititititititititititititit
itititititititititititititititit
itititititititititititititititit
itititititititititititititititit
itititititititititititititititit
itititititititititititititititit
```

This sonnet falls within the 'Pronouns' category of Andre's cycle. Focusing, as he intends, on the materiality of the word, we uncover not only 'it', but 'tit', which could belong to 'Body Parts'. Interestingly, Andre's list for that category uses 'nipple' instead. The 'Pronouns' category takes precedence in this sonnet.

# LECTURE ON NOTHING

I am here                    ,              and there is nothing to say                    .

                                                                    If among you are
those who wish to get    somewhere                    ,                    let them leave at
any moment              .                                    What we re–quire                    is
silence                    ;                    but what silence requires
            is              that I go on talking              .

                                                                    Give any one thought
                a push                    :              it falls down easily                    .
;                    but the pusher          and the pushed                    pro–duce              that enter–
tainment              called              a dis–cussion                    .
            Shall we have one later  ?

                                                    𝑚𝑝

Or                    ,      we could simply de–cide                                    not to have a dis–
cussion              .                                    What ever you like .                    But
now                                    there are silences                                    and the
words              make                    help make                                    the
silences              .

                                                                    I have nothing to say
            and I am saying it                    as I need it                                    and that is
poetry                                    as I need it              .

                This space of time                                    is organized
            .                    We need not fear these      silences, —
we may love them              .                    𝑚𝑝

                                                                    This is a composed
talk                    ,              for I am making it                    It is like a glass
            just as I make              a piece of music.                    glass
                of milk              .                    We need the                    glass
and we need the          milk                                    Or again          it is like an
empty glass                                    into which                                    at any
moment              anything                                    may be poured
.                    As we go along                    ,                    (who knows?)
                an i–dea may occur in this    talk                    .
                                    I have no idea              whether one will
                or not.                    If one does,              let it.                    Re–
                                    𝑚𝑝
gard it as something      seen                    momentarily                    ,                    as
though              from a window              while traveling                    .
If across Kansas                    ,                    then, of course,          Kansas
.                    Arizona                                    is more interesting,
almost too interesting    ,                    especially    for a New–Yorker              who is
being interested      in spite of himself      in everything.                    Now he knows he
needs                    the Kansas in him                    .                    Kansas is like
nothing on earth              ,                    and for a New Yorker    very refreshing.

Cage first delivered this 'composed talk' at the Artists' Club in New York in 1949 or 1950. At the time, he was turning to the making of music that incorporated chance elements and silence. *Lecture on Nothing* follows a strict structure: four measures in each line and twelve lines in each unit of the rhythmic structure, with a total of 48 units (the first seven shown here). Certainly not a concrete poem in the strict sense, it warrants inclusion for its variable use of white space (silence) and lone punctuation marks and its rubato-like reading – making it a 'verbivocovisual' text.

It is like an empty glass ,               nothing but wheat          ,                    o

is it corn                    ?          Does it matter which          ?

Kansas               has this about it:          at any instant,          one may leave it,

and whenever one wishes one may return to it          .

                                                   ♍

Or you may leave it     forever          and never return to it          ,

               for we pos–sess nothing          .                    Our poetry now

          is the reali–zation               that we possess          nothing

.                    Anything               therefore          is a delight

(since we do not     pos–sess it)          and thus          need not fear its loss

.               We need not destroy the     past:          it is gone;

at any moment,          it might reappear and     seem to be          and be the present

.               Would it be a               repetition?          Only if we thought we

owned it,          but since we don't,          it is free          and so are we


                                        Most anybody knows a–bout the future

          and how un–certain it is          .


                                        ♍

What I am calling          poetry          is often called          content.

I myself          have called          it form          .          It is the conti-

nuity          of a piece of music.          Continuity          today,

when it is necessary     ,               is a demonstration                    of dis-

interestedness.          That is,          it is a proof          that our delight

lies in not          pos–sessing anything          .          Each moment

presents what happens     .                    How different

this form sense is                    from that          which is bound up with

memory:          themes          and secondary themes;          their struggle;

their development;          the climax;          the recapitulation          (which is the belief

that one may          own one's own home)          .          But actually,

unlike the snail          ,          we carry our homes          within us,

                                        ♍

which enables us                    to fly                                        or to stay

, —               to enjoy          each.          But beware of

that which is          breathtakingly          beautiful,          for at any moment

          the telephone          may ring          or the airplane

come down in a          vacant lot          .          A piece of string

or a sunset          ,          possessing neither          ,

each acts               and the continuity          happens

.          Nothing more than          nothing          can be said.

Hearing          or making this          in music          is not different

—          only simpler —          than living this way          .

          Simpler, that is          ,               for me, — because it happens

               that I write music          .

                    ♍  ♍

and how un–certain it is

.

♍

What I am calling        poetry        is often called        content.

I myself        have called        it form        .        It is the conti-

nuity        of a piece of music.        Continuity        today,

when it is necessary        ,        is a demonstration        of dis-

interestedness.        That is,        it is a proof        that our delight

lies in not        pos–sessing anything        .        Each moment

presents what happens        .        How different

this form sense is        from that        which is bound up with

memory:        themes        and secondary themes;        their struggle;

their development;        the climax;        the recapitulation        (which is the belief

that one may        own one's own home)        .        But actually,

unlike the snail        ,        we carry our homes        within us,

♍

which enables us        to fly        or to stay

, —        to enjoy        each.        But beware of

that which is        breathtakingly        beautiful,        for at any moment

the telephone        may ring        or the airplane

come down in a        vacant lot        A piece of string

or a sunset        ,        possessing neither        ,

each acts        and the continuity        happens

.        Nothing more than        nothing        can be said.

Hearing        or making this        in music        is not different

—        only simpler —        than living this way        .

Simpler, that is        ,        for me, — because it happens

that I write music        .

♍  ♍

Both a sound and a concrete poet, bpNichol uses the word 'love' in this poem to explore visual permutations across the horizontal, vertical and diagonal axes of the page. 'evol', a reverse spelling of 'love', reads left to right and up to down. The repeated e's at centre and on the diagonal make the poem spin and insert the lover's joyful sound, 'eee'.

# Moon Shot Sonnet

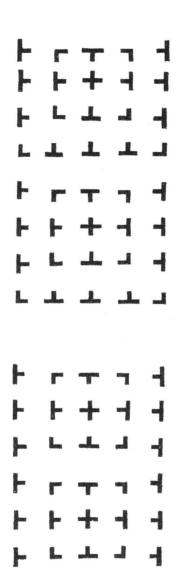

Solt writes that she copied the symbols in her sonnet from scientists' markings on the first photos of the moon published in the *New York Times*. They used fourteen 'lines' with five 'accents'. She calls her poem 'both a spoof of old forms and a statement about the necessity for new'.

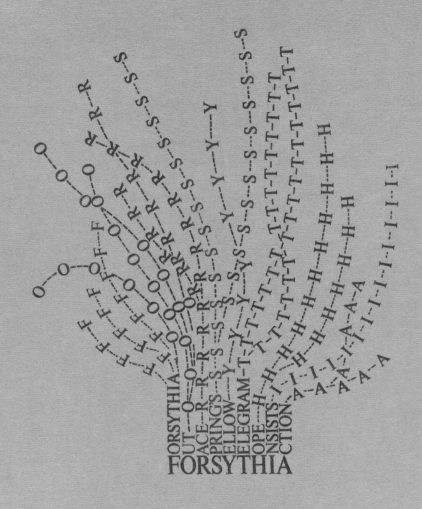

Growing out of each letter in the word FORSYTHIA is a new word which reads vertically
to produce the syntactically ambiguous word string: 'Forsythia Out Race Spring's Yellow
Telegram Hope Insists Action'. Curving fronds repeat the letters of FORSYTHIA, with dashes
between letters representing the Morse Code equivalent of the repeating letter. Solt visually
and verbally paints forsythia as a metaphoric telegram, a harbinger of spring, a missive of
hope and energy after a grey, dead winter.

This concrete poem in scroll format originated in 1962 as a performance piece called *Alphabet Symphony*. Williams assigned an object or activity to each letter of the alphabet (A: transistor radio, B: hairbrush, C: pharaoh's serpents, D: absorbent gauze, E: flute), then performed the individual letters as conductor Dick Higgins pulled them out of a hat. For the scroll, a medium Williams pioneered as a score which the performer unfurls and reads aloud, the 26 letters of the alphabet appear in long columns like numbers printed on adding-machine tape.

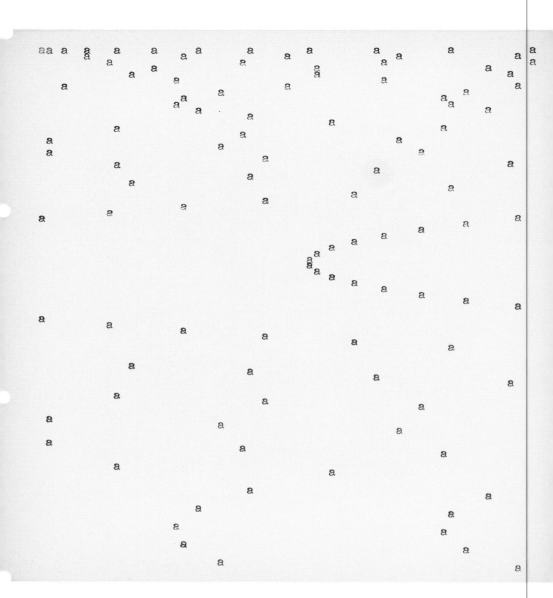

Williams approached Daniel Spoerri with a manuscript for *Material*, no. 3, which usurped a planned number by Eugen Gomringer. He derived his title, 'konkretionen' (concretions), from the unlimited possibilities of the typewriter to create surprising patterns based on the letters of the alphabet. He experimented with chance orientations ('o one') and made novel use of die-cuts that revealed letter patterns ('merdealors' – 'shit then', and '25 letters of alphabet'). Spoerri invited his friend André Thomkins to devise a unique binding for this issue, which further incorporated a die-cut cover, but left the pages loose.

one neo eon eno oen noe oe oe eo eo eo eo oe eo o o o o o o

Imperfections

a b c d e
f g h i j
k l m n o
p q r s t
u v w x y

h e

s e a t s

h e r

a t

t h e

s e a

Williams designed 'Sweethearts' as an intimate artist's book to be manipulated and experienced through movement. The text consists of a single word, 'sweethearts', the letters of which appear in different formations, starting with 'he', then 'she'. On each of the variant pages, Williams arranges, adds and omits letterforms all set in the Futura font. He indicated that the work was intended to be read from back to front and could be experienced as a flipbook, offering a cinematic experience.

# POSTLUDE

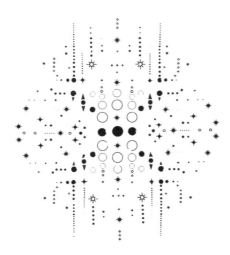

Beaulieu's concrete poetry is characterized by what he calls 'momentary eruptions of non-meaning which are then coopted back into representation by the very act of identification'. In *untitled*, he explores the fine line between legible e, o and exclamation points, and black spirals that serve an improvisatory, rhythmic function.

Beaulieu argues that contemporary concrete poetry distances itself from a universal language of advertising. His 'snowflakes', produced using dry-transfer surveyor's marks and punctuation and with an eye to radial symmetry, are a physical treatment of Allen Ginsberg's dictum 'first thought, best thought'. The rarity of the medium means that each letter or symbol once applied cannot be adjusted.

This poem visually arranges an excerpt from Louis Aragon's 'Treatise on Style' (as translated by Charles Henri Ford) to create a text which physically embodies Aragon's confrontational opinions on syntax. Beaulieu explodes reading by shifting in and out of boldface and avoiding a lineated text.

effect silk codes would have on
agents in the field, he answered that
or what shall I say to you
ifort to me that I was so separate
tage—our lives are all exceeding brittle
could hide behind the silk
In common wi*
eluctance—Remember Lot's wife

Howe describes her poetry in this artist's book as 'type-collages'. Drawing from the diary of Hannah Edwards Wetmore, the younger sister of American theologian Jonathan Edwards, Howe reproduces the entries photographically, creates her own transcriptions, renders them in different typefaces, prints them out, and cuts and tapes the printed text into collages. 'Even the "invisible" scotch tape I recently used when composing "Frolic Architecture" leaves traces on paper when I run each original sheet through the Canon copier.' For Howe, print and voice are inseparable. She imagines the 'blank space' of the page as an essential 'quiet' that 'articulates poetry'. The sound of her text becomes an audible effect, a 'vocalized wilderness'.

abiding place but ought not a confederation
anged in fair order, at no...

d sing her welcome. She along th. me
who come weary and heavy laden
What a bleak account I have drawn up against
_' ook forward Oh my soul

Howe's approach intersects with concrete poetry in its graphic presence on the page, its break with linearity and legibility, its focus on the materiality of the word or letter, and its semantic density. It differs in its use of found text, especially documentary, and its pursuit of collage. The first passage (see p. 193) repeats the word 'silk' in different contexts ('silk codes would have on', 'could hide behind the silk'). Howe implies a phonic connection between 'silk' and 'salt' ('the latter unstated, but see the line: "Remember Lot's wife"'). The second example invokes biblical language: 'who come weary and heavy laden'; 'Look forward Oh my soul'.

```
*   je sais
    j'ai su
    je suis
    jesus
```

```
*   adieu
    a dieu
    a qui?
    ¿aqui?
```

```
*   change:

    o  yourself
    o  your life
    o  the world

    (you will only make matters worse)
    hommage à john cage & chinese thinkers
```

```
*   insecurity
    in security
```

```
*   war was
    was war
    was war?
    war war
    war was?
    war was
    here.
```

```
*   here now
    hero new
    now here
    how near
```

```
*   la frontière entre ça et ça et ça et ça et ça
```

```
*   gold mine

    l'or
    loro
    leur
    l'heure
    l'horreur
```

```
*   beast beats beauty
    beats beast beats
    beauty beats beast
```

```
*   macht
    lacht
    sacht:
    nacht.
      ach!
```

```
*   no moral
    no mor al
    nor o, mal
    normal
```

```
*       get
    target
    &
      r  e
        g
      r et.
```

```
*   peace piece:

    peace,
    please.
```

```
*   you could be honest with everyone
    you could lie to everyone
    you could confuse both
```

Rinne's concrete poetry highlights multiple languages through puns. Her minimalist poem opens with the rhyming 'j'ai su' (I knew) and 'jesus' (French), continues with an alternation between the German words 'war' (was) and 'was' (what), where both words also have English meanings, and subsequently presents the French 'l'or' (gold) as it evolves sonically into 'leur' (their) and the rhyming 'l'horreur' (horror). Such sonic affinities call for a performative reading with text in hand.

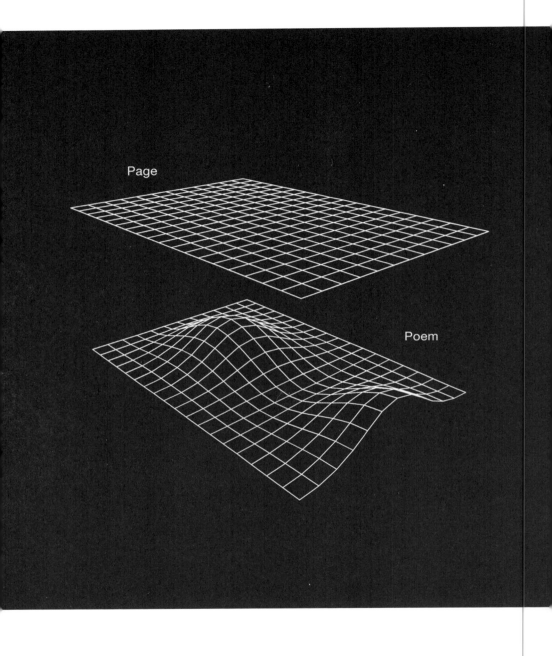

This poem's title is an excerpt from unfinished notes for a treatise on linguistics by Mallarmé (1869) – 'We did not understand Descartes'. The sine wave form of Vallias's 'poem' allows him to make a diagrammatic gesture in three-dimensional space. Poetry is thus set free from the domain of the page.

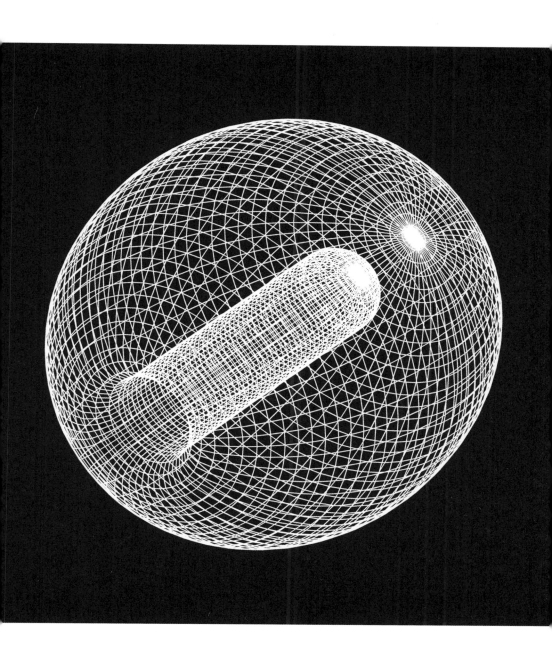

'Io' is Italian for the first-person pronoun, 'I'. It is also the acronym for Input/Output. Vallias shows the lowercase 'i' penetrating the sphere, which is the letter 'o'. In the artist's interactive version (no longer functional), the opaque sphere turns around on a continuous 'o' background sound, then becomes transparent as the sound changes to a continuous 'i'. In the passage from opacity to transparency, we hear the dipthong 'oi'; from transparency to opacity, the dipthong 'io'.

# BIOGRAPHIES

**Friedrich Achleitner** (Austrian, 1930–2019)
Born in Schalchen, Upper Austria, Achleitner studied architecture at the Academy of Fine Arts Vienna from 1950 to 1953. In 1955 he joined the Wiener Gruppe, consisting of the poets H. C. Artmann, Konrad Bayer, Gerhard Rühm and Oswald Wiener. Achleitner participated in the group's literary cabarets and wrote concrete poems, as well as poems in the Viennese dialect. He began working as an architecture critic in 1961 and enjoyed a prestigious career as a university professor of the history and theory of architecture, including publication of five volumes of his *Österreichische Architektur im 20. Jahrhundert* (1980–2010).

**Jeremy Adler** (British, b. 1947)
Jeremy Adler is a British scholar and poet, and Emeritus Professor and Senior Research Fellow at King's College London. As a poet he is known especially for his concrete poetry and artist's books.

**Carl Andre** (American, b. 1935)
Born in Quincy, Massachusetts, Andre studied art at Phillips Academy in Andover, Massachusetts. After serving in the u.s. Army from 1955 to 1956, he moved to New York City in 1956. Through his Phillips Academy friend the filmmaker and theoretician Hollis Frampton, Andre met the Romanian sculptor Constantin Brancusi, who introduced him to a former Phillips classmate, the painter Frank Stella. Impressed by what he called Stella's 'constructivist' technique of building up work from 'identical, discrete units',

Andre applied this technique to concrete poems which he wrote between 1960 and 1964, while working as freight brakeman and conductor in New Jersey for the Pennsylvania Railroad. Since the late 1960s Andre has often exhibited the manuscripts of these text-based works alongside his mature sculptures. From his first public exhibition at the Tibor de Nagy Gallery in 1965, he has achieved fame as one of the most widely recognized minimalist sculptors.

**Ronaldo Azeredo** (Brazilian, 1937–2006)
The poet Azeredo joined the Brazilian movement of concrete poetry, known as Noigandres, in 1956. He contributed the poem *z* to the National Concrete Art Exhibition in São Paulo in 1956 and the poster poem *Velocidade* to the fourth issue of the literary magazine *Noigandres.*

**Konrad Bayer** (Austrian, 1932–1964)
Bayer was an Austrian writer and poet and a member of the Wiener Gruppe, in the company of Friedrich Achleitner, H. C. Artmann, Gerhard Rühm and Oswald Wiener. His work combined an array of disparate influences, including Dadaism, surrealism, pataphysics and the philosophical poetics of Wittgenstein. Bayer's most important works are the novels *Der Kopf des Vitus Bering* (The Head of Vitus Bering) and *Der sechste Sinn* (The Sixth Sense), published posthumously in 1965 and 1966. He committed suicide in October 1964 at the age of 32.

**Derek Beaulieu** (Canadian, b. 1973)
Beaulieu is a poet, publisher and anthologist. He studied contemporary Canadian poetics at the University of Calgary and Creative Writing at Roehampton University, London. His work has appeared internationally in small press publications, magazines and visual art galleries. He founded and directed 'housepress' from 1997 to 2004. In 2005, he co-edited *Shift and Switch: New Canadian Poetry*, a controversial anthology that has been reviewed internationally. Beaulieu lives in Banff, Alberta, where he is Director of Literary Arts at the Banff Centre for Arts and Creativity.

**Max Bense** (German, 1910–1990)
Bense was a German philosopher, writer and publicist known for
his work in the philosophy of science, logic, aesthetics and semiotics.
In 1949 he was appointed guest professor in philosophy at the
University of Stuttgart. Between 1954 and 1958 he responded to
a request from the concrete artist Max Bill to teach 'information'
at the Ulm School of Design. In Stuttgart, his literary group
consisted of the philosophers and writers Reinhard Dohl, Ludwig
Harig and Helmut Heissenbüttel and the typographers Hansjörg
Mayer and Klaus Burkhardt.

**Edgard Braga** (Brazilian, 1897–1985)
Braga graduated with a medical degree in Rio de Janeiro and worked
as an obstetrician. He published his first book of poetry in 1933, and
in the 1960s he joined the editorial team of the magazine of avant-
garde poetry *Invenção*, directed by Décio Pignatari. Ian Hamilton
Finlay published Braga's poem *Example 1* on the cover of *Poor.Old.
Tired.Horse*. no. 21.

**Claus Bremer** (German, 1924–1996)
Bremer, a German dramatist, participated in the founding of the
Darmstadt Circle of Concrete Poetry in 1957. He joined the group's
leader, the Romanian-born poet Daniel Spoerri, and the American
expatriate Emmett Williams in publishing the concrete poetry
magazine *Material* between 1957 and 1959. Eugen Gomringer
credited Bremer with having 'enriched' the constellation form. His
'engagierende texte' ('engaged texts') encourage the reader to make
his/her own interpretation of the poem by becoming engaged in the
process of its structure.

**John Cage** (American, 1912–1992)
Cage was an American composer, music theorist and philosopher
and a pioneer of musical indeterminacy, electroacoustic music and
the non-traditional use of musical instruments. He is considered one
of the seminal composers of the twentieth century. After graduating
from Los Angeles High School, he enrolled at Pomona College
in Claremont in 1928, then dropped out in 1930 and travelled in
Europe through 1931. His music teachers upon returning to the

United States included Henry Cowell (1933), Richard Buhlig (early 1930s) and Arnold Schoenberg (1933–5), and he became a disciple of East and South Asian cultures, which he first encountered while working as piano accompanist at the Cornish School in Seattle in 1938–40. At the Cornish School he also introduced the prepared piano. Through his studies of Indian philosophy and Zen Buddhism in the late 1940s in New York City, Cage invented musical composition based on chance operations, which he started to pursue in 1951 using the I Ching (Book of Changes). The I Ching was to be central to his music for the rest of his life, whether working with his silent piece, 4'33" (1952) or with graphic notation.

**Henri Chopin** (French, 1922–2008)
Born in Paris, Chopin was a leading practitioner of concrete and sound poetry. The graphic works he created on his typewriter, known as typewriter poems, often have a sound component. Chopin was also the producer of original recordings using early tape recorders, studio technologies and the sounds of the manipulated human voice. In 1964 he founded OU, one of the most important reviews of the second half of the twentieth century, which he ran until 1974. Each issue contained recordings, texts, images, screenprints and multiples. Among the contributors were William S. Burroughs, François Dufrêne, Bernard Heidsieck and the Dada poet and visual artist Raoul Hausmann.

**Bob Cobbing** (British, 1920–2002)
Born in Enfield, England, Cobbing first trained as an accountant, then as a teacher. His early interest in performance led to his creation of Writers Forum, a small publisher, workshop and writers' network which began publishing in 1963. Around this time, Cobbing left teaching and managed Better Books, a stage, cinema and alternative gallery that embraced assemblage, performance art and radical poetry. During the first half of the 1970s he used the facilities of the Poetry Society to produce Writers Forum books by British Revival poets and by John Cage, Allen Ginsberg and Ian Hamilton Finlay. He pursued his interest in performance for multiple voices until his death.

**Augusto de Campos** (Brazilian, b. 1931)
Born in São Paulo, poet, visual artist, translator and literary and
music critic Augusto de Campos joined his brother Haroldo and
their university friend Décio Pignatari in launching the literary
magazine *Noigandres*, and in founding the Noigandres group,
which initiated the international movement of concrete poetry in
Brazil. Noigandres's pivotal manifesto, *Pilot Plan for Concrete Poetry*
(1958), utilized James Joyce's term 'verbivocovisual' to indicate
that the visual, sonic and semantic dimensions of a poem could
not be separated. Beginning in 1980, Augusto experimented with
new media by presenting his poems in digital form, on video, using
neon and computer graphics, and involving sound and music. His
collaboration with his son, Cid Campos, from 1987 to the present
day, has resulted in POESIA É RISCO (Poetry is Risk), a CD started by
PolyGram in 1995 that developed into a multimedia performance.
As a translator of poetry, Augusto has specialized in the work of
avant-garde poets Ezra Pound, Joyce, Gertrude Stein and e. e.
cummings, as well as the Russians Vladimir Mayakovsky and Velimir
Khlebnikov. He is a recipient of the Pablo Neruda Poetry Prize in
Chile (2015) and the Janus Pannonius Grand Prize for Poetry in
Hungary (2017).

**Haroldo de Campos** (Brazilian, 1929–2003)
Haroldo de Campos, a Brazilian poet, critic, professor and
translator, is considered one of the most important figures in
Brazilian literature since 1950. He joined his brother Augusto and
their university friend Décio Pignatari in founding the experimental
poetry journal *Noigandres*, which launched the Brazilian concrete
poetry movement in 1955. At this time, Haroldo also introduced
the new Brazilian poetry to Japanese avant-garde poets. Best
known for his monumental prose poem *Galáxias* (published 1984),
Haroldo likewise contributed highly influential theoretical essays
such as 'Concrete Poetry – Language – Communication' and 'Poetic
Function and Ideogram/The Sinological Argument'. In addition,
he translated significant literature of the Western tradition into
Portuguese, including Homer's *Iliad*, prose by James Joyce, poetry
by Stéphane Mallarmé, and work by Dante, Goethe, Vladimir
Mayakovsky, Octavio Paz and Ezra Pound.

**Paul De Vree** (Belgian, 1909–1982)

De Vree worked as a draughtsman and painter in an advertising agency. He founded the Belgian literary journal *De Tafelronde* (1955–82), which under his leadership became the major advocate for concrete and visual poetry in Flanders. With the Italian poet Sarenco, De Vree also founded and directed *Lotta Poetica* (1971–5), a magazine of the international visual poetry movement in Italy. De Vree's best known audio-visual poems, such as *Vertigo Gli*, *Kleine Caroli* and *Veronika*, were recorded and released on vinyl record, with liner notes by Henri Chopin, as a supplement to *Lotta Poetica* no. 4.

**Ian Hamilton Finlay** (Scottish, 1925–2006)

A poet, writer, visual artist and AVANT-GARDEner, Finlay was born in Nassau, the Bahamas, and sent to boarding school in Scotland when he was six. Between 1944 and 1947 he served with the Non-combatant and Service Corps, then lived in rural Scotland and on the Orkney Islands. From 1956 onwards, Finlay was based largely in Edinburgh. He set up his Wild Hawthorn Press in spring 1961, and a year later the press launched the periodical *Poor.Old.Tired.Horse.*, printing rural Scottish lyrics alongside contemporary international poets. In late 1962 Finlay's career shifted dramatically when he encountered the work of the Brazilian concrete poetry group Noigandres. Within a year he had featured the poetry of Augusto de Campos in POTH and had published his first collection of concrete poetry, *Rapel: Ten Fauve and Suprematist Poems*. Over the next three decades, Finlay and his wife Sue built up the grounds of the farmstead Stonypath, Dunsyre, into an interactive poetic landscape, which he christened Little Sparta in the late 1970s. From then until his death, Finlay created installations of sculpture, emblems and poetry both in Little Sparta and in gardens around the world.

**Heinz Gappmayr** (Austrian, 1925–2010)

Gappmayr was an artist from Innsbruck who created works of visual poetry. He was among the artist-theoreticians whose texts and artworks focused since the 1960s on the connections between the visual and linguistic production of meaning. Gappmayr relies on geometric shapes as 'signs' to convey 'notions'. Some of his poems express their messages by means of a black square, but he also uses words apart from geometric design. To him 'concrete' means all conditions of language.

**Matthias Goeritz** (German-born Mexican, 1915–1990)
Goeritz was a Mexican painter and sculptor of German origin. He spent his childhood in Berlin and pursued philosophy and the history of art at the Friedrich-Wilhelms-Universität in Bonn, while also studying art at the Berlin-Charlottenburg School of Arts and Crafts. In early 1941, during the Second World War, Goeritz left Germany, settling first in Morocco, then in Spain and finally in Mexico, where he was offered a position as an art history teacher. During the 1950s Goeritz collaborated with the architect Luis Barragán to produce massive, abstract concrete sculptures. He called his first concrete poems (*c.* 1959) *Mensajes* (Messages), after a series of gold-plated sculptures on wood.

**Eugen Gomringer** (Bolivian-born German, b. 1925)
The son of a Bolivian mother and a Swiss father, Gomringer grew up in Switzerland where he studied art history and economics. As one of the founders of the concrete poetry movement, he edited and published the Swiss-based journal *Konkrete Poesie Poesia Concreta,* featuring work by Heissenbüttel, Rühm, Bremer, Gullar, Jandl and Morgan. In 2000 he established the Institute for Constructive Art and Concrete Poetry in Rehau, southern Germany, where he now lives.

**José Lino Grünewald** (Brazilian, 1931–2000)
Grünewald was a multi-disciplinary intellectual and member of the Noigandres group of Brazilian concrete poets. He contributed to *Noigandres* 5 in 1962 and worked on the *Invenção* magazine. His talents included poetry, translation (especially Ezra Pound's *The Cantos*), and critical essays (major works compiled in O *Grau Zero Do Escreviver*, organized by José Guilherme Corrêa, published in São Paulo, 2002).

**Ferreira Gullar** (Brazilian, 1930–2016)
Ferreira Gullar, the pen name of the Brazilian poet, playwright, essayist and art critic José Ribamar Ferreira, was exiled to Argentina by the Brazilian dictatorship that lasted from 1964 until 1985. He played an important role in the formation of the Neo-Concrete movement, which opposed the geometric, rational theory of concrete art in favour of an expressive phenomenology that invites the participation of the spectator.

**Dom Sylvester Houédard** (British, 1924–1992)
Born in Guernsey, an island in the English Channel off the coast of Normandy, Houédard was educated at Jesus College, Oxford, served in British Army Intelligence from 1944 to 1947 and was ordained a priest in 1959, taking the name Dom (an honorific for Benedictine monks). Best known for the typewriter-composed visual poems he called 'typestracts', Houédard was a leading proponent of concrete poetry, contributing regularly to magazines and exhibitions from the early 1960s onwards.

**Susan Howe** (American, b. 1937)
Howe is an American poet, scholar, essayist and critic. Born in Boston, she graduated from the Boston Museum School of Fine Arts in 1961 and moved to New York to pursue painting. In 1988 she had her first visiting professorship in English at the University of Buffalo, the State University of New York, and was later appointed Capen Chair and Distinguished Professor. Howe has also held the position of Distinguished Fellow at the Stanford Institute of the Humanities. Pursuing what she calls 'type-collages', Howe reproduces found texts photographically, renders them in different typefaces, and cuts and tapes the printed text into collages. Among her awards, she is a recipient of the Yale Bollingen Prize in American Poetry (2011) and Canada's Griffin Poetry Prize (2018).

**Ernst Jandl** (Austrian, 1925–2000)
An Austrian writer, poet and translator, Jandl became known for his experimental poetry, principally sound poems designed in the tradition of concrete poetry. Born in Vienna, Jandl was drafted

into the German Army in 1943 and detained in an American prison camp until 1946. After the war, he studied German philology and in 1950 wrote his doctoral thesis on the short stories of Arthur Schnitzler. Jandl completed his teaching certification in 1949 and worked as a teacher until 1979. In autumn 1971 he was a Visiting German Writer at the University of Texas at Austin. In 1977 he gave six lectures about new poetry at the Technische Universität Wien.

**Kitasono Katue** (Japanese, 1902–1978)
Among twentieth-century Japanese poets, Katue was the one best known in Europe and the United States. Active from the mid-1920s, he was first entranced by Dadaism and Surrealism, then absorbed by the ideas of Futurism, Cubism, Abstract Expressionism and Minimalism. He served as an editor and graphic designer for poetry and visual art journals, including his own *vou*, which he published from 1935 to 1940 and then again from 1945 until his death. His 'plastic poems', created using a camera to photograph newspaper print, Styrofoam and photographs, became his own form of visual poetry.

**Ferdinand Kriwet** (German, 1942–2018)
Kriwet was a multimedia artist and poet who produced several major audio programmes for West German public radio. These *Hörtexte* (audio texts) are collages of noise, soundbites and samples appropriated from television and radio. Kriwet's most famous *Sehtexte* (visual texts) are the *Rundscheiben* (round discs). These poster-size, circular prints, shown at exhibitions and on billboards, contain texts that challenge a linear reading. Kriwet wrote about the *Rundscheiben* in his book *Leserattenfänge. Sehtextkommentare* (Bookworm Trappings. Visual Text Commentary, 1965).

**Hansjörg Mayer** (German, b. 1943)
Poet, typographer and publisher Hansjörg Mayer is best known as the publisher of 75 titles in the 1960s, including three major concrete poetry portfolios in 1964, 1965 and 1966, each featuring thirteen poets. Raised in Stuttgart to a family of typographers, Mayer studied information aesthetics, philosophy of technology and semiotics with Max Bense. Experiments in the form

and presentation of individual letters became the focus of his sequence of portfolios and prints that were later dubbed 'typoems' by the Brazilian poet Haroldo de Campos. Mayer's small-press, independent imprint Edition Hansjörg Mayer, set up in 1964, was associated with the Futura typeface. He taught at the Bath Academy of Art in the late 1960s and lives in England to the present day.

**Franz Mon** (German, b. 1926)
Mon studied German, history and philosophy in Frankfurt am Main and Freiburg im Breisgau. In 1959 he published his first collection of poetry and essays, *artikulationen* (Articulations). The following year, he edited the *movens* anthology with Walter Höllerer and Manfred de la Motte, before founding Typos Press in 1962 to publish works of concrete and visual poetry. Mon taught graphic design in Kassel, Karlsruhe and at the Hochschule für Gestaltung Offenbach am Main. In his visual texts, he sets out to prove that there exists 'the possibility of a spatially rather than temporally articulated written language'.

**Edwin Morgan** (Scottish, 1920–2010)
Morgan is widely recognized as one of the foremost Scottish poets of the twentieth century. In 1937 he entered the University of Glasgow, where he studied French and Russian and taught himself Italian and German. After interrupting his studies to serve in the Second World War as a non-combatant conscientious objector with the Royal Army Medical Corps, Morgan graduated in 1947 and became a lecturer at the university. He retired as a full professor in 1980. Morgan worked in a wide range of styles, from the sonnet to concrete poetry. His exceptional talents as a translator inspired ingenious interpretations of the great Russian Futurist poets into Scots.

**Barrie Phillip Nichol** (known as **bpNichol**, Canadian, 1944–1988) was a writer, sound poet and editor whose work encompassed not only poetry, but children's books, television scripts, novels, short fiction and computer texts. Born in Vancouver, British Columbia, he first received recognition in the 1960s for concrete poetry. As a sound poet, he joined the group of Canadian poets called The Four Horsemen (active 1972–88), which comprised, in addition to bpNichol, Rafael Barreto-Rivera, Paul Dutton and Steve McCaffery. They were known for their performances of concrete as well as sound poetry.

### Sei'ichi Niikuni (Japanese, 1925–1977)

A poet and painter, Niikuni was one of the foremost leaders of the international concrete poetry movement. Born in Sendai, Miyagi Prefecture, Niikuni studied architecture at the Sendai Technical School and English literature at the Tohoku Gakuin University. Graduating in 1951, he moved to Tokyo in 1962. In 1964 he established the *Association of Study of Arts* and its namesake magazine, which published both Japanese and foreign concrete poetry and translated poems by Haroldo de Campos into Japanese. In the mid-1960s, Niikuni met the Brazilian poet (and Noigandres member) Luis Carlos Vinholes and through him the French poet Pierre Garnier. In 1974 he held a solo exhibition at the Whitechapel Art Gallery in London.

### Décio Pignatari (Brazilian, 1927–2012)

Pignatari was a poet, designer and translator. Born in Jundiaí, Brazil, he began his experiments with poetic language in the 1950s by incorporating visual elements and the fragmentation of words. He met Augusto and Haroldo de Campos at the University of São Paulo Law Faculty and, together, they broke from what Pignatari described as the 'post-war lyrical jargon: vegetative, reactionary' to form the Noigandres group and its journal of the same name, launched in 1952. In 1958 in *Noigandres 4*, the three Brazilians published their manifesto, *Pilot Plan for Concrete Poetry*. Pignatari went on to produce translations of Marshall McLuhan, Dante, Goethe and Shakespeare.

### Cia Rinne (Swedish-Finnish, b. 1973)

Rinne studied philosophy, history and foreign languages at the universities of Frankfurt, Athens and Helsinki. Born in Sweden into a Finnish family and raised in Germany, she holds an MA

in philosophy from Helsinki. Rinne writes visual poetry and

conceptual pieces using different languages. Her publications include *zaroum* (Helsinki, 2001), the online work *archives zaroum* (2008) and the book *notes for soloists* (Stockholm, 2009). In Germany, she is best known for her documentary book *Die Romareisen* (The Rome Trips), which she published with the photographer Joakim Eskildsen.

**Dieter Roth** (Swiss, 1930–1998)
Born Karl-Dietrich Roth in Hannover, Germany, Roth trained as a graphic artist in Switzerland. In 1953 he joined the Swiss designer Marcel Wyss and the Bolivian-born German poet Eugen Gomringer in co-founding the magazine *Spirale*, which published concrete poetry and original prints. In 1954 Roth met the Swiss artist Daniel Spoerri, who invited him to produce the second issue of his new concrete poetry magazine, *Material* (January 1959). Among the artists' books Roth published in the late 1950s and '60s while living in Iceland was *Bok* (Book), which used cut holes and the option to rearrange the pages in any order. In 1964 he visited New York where he established contact with key Fluxus artists.

**Gerhard Rühm** (Austrian, b. 1930)
A poet, composer and visual artist, Rühm studied piano and music composition at the University of Music and Performing Arts Vienna in the early 1950s. At the same time, he took private lessons with the twelve-tone composer Josef Mathias Hauer. In 1952 Rühm produced his first visual works in the form of spiral and wave drawings. He met the writers Hans Carl Artmann and Konrad Bayer, the musician Oswald Wiener and the architect Friedrich Achleitner, founding with them the Wiener Gruppe in 1954. The Wiener Gruppe's intermedia and performative approach anticipated important twentieth-century artistic trends such as happenings. After Konrad Bayer committed suicide in 1964, the group broke up. Together with his Austrian fellow artists and Dieter Roth, Rühm organized a series of poetry workshops in the 1970s. In 1972 he was invited to assume the position of Professor of Free Graphics at the State Academy of Fine Arts Hamburg, a position he held until his retirement in 1996. In 2013 he was awarded the Austrian Decoration for Science and Art.

**Mary Ellen Solt** (American, 1920–2007)
Born in Gilmore City, Iowa, Solt earned a BA in literature at
Iowa State Teachers College and an MA at the University of Iowa.
She began writing concrete poetry in the 1960s and edited her
influential anthology, *Concrete Poetry: A World View*, in 1968. Her
poetry collections include *Flowers in Concrete* (1966), *Marriage: A
Code Poem* (1976), and *The Peoplemover, 1968: A Demonstration Poem*
(1978). Solt was Professor Emeritus at Indiana University at the
time of her death.

**Daniel Spoerri** (Swiss, b. Romania 1930)
Spoerri is best known for his book *Topographie Anécdotée du Hasard*
(1960), in which he mapped all the objects located on his table at a
particular moment, describing each with his personal recollections.
In 1966 Emmett Williams published an English translation with
the subtitle *Re-anecdoted Version*, and Dieter Roth later produced
a German edition. In 1958–9 Spoerri published the concrete
poetry magazine *Material*, featuring work by Bremer, Gomringer,
Roth, Williams and others. He founded his Editions MAT, which
established the medium now recognized as the multiple, in 1959.

**André Vallias** (Brazilian, b. 1963)
Vallias received his graduate education in law at the University
of São Paulo. In the early 1980s he studied proportions in art
by developing a series of black-and-white drawings based on
strict mathematical principles. In 1985 he began to design visual
poems. From 1987 to 1994 he lived in Germany, where he shifted
his activities towards translation and computer media. In 1992
he organized, together with Friedrich W. Block, one of the first
international shows of computer-generated poetry, 'poesie-digitale
dichtkunst', in Annaberg-Buchholz, Germany. Today he lives in Rio
de Janeiro.

**Edgardo Antonio Vigo** (Argentine, 1928–1997)
Visual artist Vigo was born in the small city of La Plata, a few
kilometres from Buenos Aires. The son of a carpenter, he graduated
from the Escuela Superior de Bellas Artes of La Plata with a degree
in drawing. Subsequently, Vigo travelled to Europe, where he came

into contact with the international avant-garde. He developed an extensive network, making La Plata a hub of the mail art movement. Vigo's visual poems contain symbols to be interpreted by the reader. His inclusion in Argentina's Pavilion for the 1994 São Paulo Biennial solidified his position in Latin American conceptual art.

**Emmett Williams** (American, 1925–2007)
Born in Greenville, South Carolina, the poet and visual artist Williams studied poetry with John Crowe Ransom at Kenyon College and took courses in anthropology at the University of Paris. Williams joined Daniel Spoerri and Claus Bremer as a member of the Darmstadt circle of concrete poetry (1957–9) and contributed to their concrete poetry magazine *Material*. He collaborated with the Fluxus artists Benjamin Patterson, Robert Filliou and Dieter Roth and published his long, erotic concrete poem *Sweethearts* with Edition Hansjörg Mayer in 1967. He and his wife, the British visual artist Ann Noël, moved permanently to Berlin in 1980. In 1991 he published an autobiography, *My Life in Fluxus – And Vice Versa*, with Edition Hansjörg Mayer.

**Pedro Xisto** (Brazilian, 1901–1987)
Xisto worked as a state prosecutor and cultural attaché in Brazil. He started producing haiku in 1949, and in 1957 he wrote criticism on concrete poetry for the São Paulo daily newspaper. Xisto became a member of the editorial board of the magazine *Invenção*, published by the Noigandres (1962–7). His work principally explored elements of traditional Japanese poetry and its ideograms and was included in an exhibition of Brazilian concrete poetry organized by the Brazilian poet L. C. Vinholes at the National Museum of Modern Art in Tokyo in 1960.

# REFERENCES

For the poetry by Augusto de Campos, translations from the Portuguese are by Augusto. The translation of 'sos' is by Marjorie Perloff.

1 The poem *Rever* was published in 1964. For a short video of the exhibition of the same name, see www.youtube.com/watch?v=_ZfQZpyR0mQ, first posted 17 November 2016.
2 See Marcelo Ferraz, 'The Making of sesc Pompéia', http://linabobarditogether.com, 3 August 2012.
3 See Johanna Drucker, 'Experimental, Visual, and Concrete Poetry: A Note on Historical Context and Basic Concepts', in *Experimental – Visual – Concrete: Avant-garde Poetry Since the 1960s*, ed. K. David Jackson, Eric Vos and Johanna Drucker (Amsterdam and Atlanta, GA, 1996), p. 39.
4 The points on concrete and visual poetry are culled from 'The Yale *Symphosymposium* on Contemporary Poetics and Concretism: A World View from the 1990s', in *Experiment – Visual – Concrete*, ed. Jackson, Vos and Drucker, comments by Marjorie Perloff (p. 374), Charles Bernstein (p. 392) and John Solt (p. 399). For examples of visual poetry, see *The New Concrete: Visual Poetry in the 21st Century*, ed. Victoria Bean and Chris McCabe (London, 2015).
5 Kenneth Goldsmith, 'Make It New: Post-digital Concrete Poetry in the 21st Century', in *The New Concrete*, ed. Bean and McCabe, p. 15.
6 Jackson, Vos and Drucker, eds, *Experiment – Visual – Concrete*, p. 385.
7 See Harris Feinsod, 'Sound Poetry', in *The Princeton Encyclopedia of Poetry and Poetics*, ed. Roland Greene and Stephen Cushman, 4th edn (Princeton, NJ, 2012), p. 1327.

8  Steve McCaffery and bpNichol, eds, *Sound Poetry: A Catalogue* (Toronto, 1978), pp. 6ff.

9  For this quotation from the manifesto *New Ways of the Word* [*the Language of the Future, Death to Symbolism*] (September 1913), see *Russian Futurism through Its Manifestos, 1912–1928*, trans. and ed. Anna Lawton and Herbert Eagle (Ithaca, NY, 1988), p. 71.

10  See Filippo Tommaso Marinetti, 'Après la Marne, Joffre visita le front en auto' (After the Marne, Joffre Visited the Front by Car), in *Les mots en liberté futuristes* (Milan, 1919).

11  Nancy Perloff, 'Sound Poetry and the Musical Avant-garde: A Musicologist's Perspective', in *The Sound of Poetry / The Poetry of Sound*, ed. Marjorie Perloff and Craig Dworkin (Chicago, IL, 2009), pp. 97–8.

12  Rosmarie Waldrop, *Dissonance (If You Are Interested)* (Tuscaloosa, AL, 2005), p. 47.

13  Teddy Hultberg, *Öyvind Fahlström on the Air – Manipulating the World* (Stockholm, 1999), p. 108. Fahlström added the subtitle when he reprinted the manifesto in *Bord-Dikter 1952–55* (Stockholm, 1966).

14  See Hultberg, *Öyvind Fahlström*, p. 109. The second epigraph translates as: 'Replace the psychology of man with THE LYRICAL OBSESSION OF MATTER.' This famous manifesto was first printed as a leaflet in French and Italian. For an excellent summary of its contents, see Marjorie Perloff, *Unoriginal Genius: Poetry by Other Means in the New Century* (Chicago, IL, 2010), p. 54.

15  This passage from his manifesto is printed ibid., p. 118.

16  Quoted ibid., p. 52. Fahlström would later call his composition 'Birds in Sweden' – produced at the Swedish Radio studios in October 1962 – 'a one-man happening for radio' (*Ord & Bild*, 2 (1964)) and 'a poem, a collage for tape'. See ibid., p. 103, n. 67.

17  From a transcript of the radio programme *Tidsspegeln*, 15 October 1964, Swedish Radio Document Archives, Stockholm. Quoted ibid., p. 24 and documented p. 97, n. 24. I should note that the argument for Fahlström's influence on concrete poetry has been contested by Augusto de Campos, who emphasizes that Fahlström did not add the subtitle 'Manifesto of Concrete Poetry' to his Swedish text until 1966, long after the publication of Augusto's *Poetamenos* (Minuspoet) in 1955.

18  For this account, see Mary Ellen Solt, *Concrete Poetry: A World View* (Bloomington, IL, 1968), p. 8.

19  *From Line to Constellation* was first published in Max Bense's magazine *Augenblick* in 1955, followed the same year by its publication in *Spirale*. See Haroldo de Campos, 'Brazilian and German Avant-garde Poetry', in *Novas: Selected Writings by Haroldo de Campos*, ed. and with an intro. by Antonio Sergio Bessa and Odile Cisneros, foreword by Roland Greene (Evanston, IL, 2007), p. 251; 373 n. 2. Quoted from Salt, *Concrete Poetry*, p. 67.

20  Translated by Mike Weaver in *Image* (1964), reprinted ibid., p. 67.

21  Reprinted ibid., pp. 68–9.

22  Haroldo de Campos, 'Anthropophagous Reason: Dialogue and Difference in Brazilian Culture', in *Novas,* ed. Bessa and Cisneros, p. 171. See also p. 222.

23  In troubadour context, this might have referred to an odour of a flower that could drive ennui away and carried sexual implications. For the etymology of 'noigandres', see Marjorie Perloff, *Unoriginal Genius: Poetry by Other Means in the New Century* (Chicago, IL, 2010), p. 179, n. 31.

24  João Bandeira and Lenora de Barros, eds, *Poesia concreta: O projeto verbivocovisual* (São Paulo, 2008), p. 14.

25  See Augusto de Campos, 'Preface' to *Poetamenos* (Minuspoet), trans. Jon M. Tolman (São Paulo, 1973). Reprinted in Sergio Bessa, 'Sound as Subject: Augusto de Campos's *Poetamenos*', in *The Sound of Poetry / The Poetry of Sound*, ed. Marjorie Perloff and Craig Dworkin (Chicago, IL, 2009), pp. 222–3.

26  Bandeira and de Barros, eds, *Poesia concreta*, p. 21.

27  At the 'First National Exhibition of Concrete Art' at the Museum of Modern Art in São Paulo, where concrete poetry was officially launched, poster-poems by the Noigandres group hung alongside paintings and sculptures by artists from São Paulo and Rio de Janeiro. The third issue of *Noigandres*, bearing the subtitle 'Concrete Poetry', was also introduced at this exhibition. See Bandeira and de Barros, eds, *Poesia concreta*, pp. 21, 24.

28  For Augusto's account of the meeting with Gomringer and its aftermath, see Augusto de Campos, 'Interview with Sergio Bessa' (unpublished, *c.* 2015). Courtesy Augusto de Campos.

The decision to use the term 'concrete poetry' is also recorded in Gomringer's essay 'The First Years of Concrete Poetry', which appeared in English in *Form*, 4 (April 1967), and in German in his collected works, *Worte sind Schatten* (1969). My thanks to Stephen Bann for this reference.

29  Quoted ibid.

30  The manifesto was published in Portuguese in *Noigandres*, no. 4.

31  Excerpted from Augusto de Campos, Décio Pignatari and Haroldo de Campos, *Plano piloto para poesia concreta* [1958], trans. in *Poesia concreta*, ed. Bandeira and de Barros, p. 90.

32  See Haroldo de Campos, 'Concrete Poetry – Language – Communication', in *Novas*, p. 245. See the commentary on Pignatari's 'Terra' in this anthology.

33  In a conversation I conducted with Rühm, he explained that they used the term 'cabaret' rather than 'experimental poetry' so as not to arouse suspicion. Unpublished transcript, Vienna, 12 June 2018.

34  For this history, see Peter Weibel, 'Preface', in *Die Wiener Gruppe / The Vienna Group: A Moment of Modernity, 1954–1960: The Visual Works and the Actions (Friedrich Achleitner, H.C. Artmann, Konrad Bayer, Gerhard Rühm, Oswald Wiener)*, ed. Peter Weibel (Vienna and New York, 1997), p. 15.

35  Rühm uses the term 'typo-collage' to mean letters appropriated from magazines and pasted on to paper. See Gerhard Rühm, *total ansicht/total view: Gerhard Rühm Retrospective, 1952–2015* (Graz, 2016), p. 91.

36  Gerhard Rühm, 'The Phenomenon of the "Wiener Gruppe" in the Vienna of the Fifties and Sixties', in *Die Wiener Gruppe*, ed. Weibel, p. 20.

37  On the meeting with Gomringer, see ibid., p. 24.

38  Gerhard Rühm, 'Konkrete Poesie', in Gerhard Rühm, *Aspekte einer erweiterten Poetik, Vorlesungen und Aufsätze* (Berlin, 2009), p. 40 (my translation).

39  Ibid.

40  Ernst Jandl and Ian Hamilton Finlay, *Not a Concrete Pot: Briefwechsel, 1964–1985*, ed. Vanessa Hannesschläger, trans. Barbara Sternthal in collaboration with Vanessa Hannesschläger (Vienna, 2017), p. 100. Jandl does not seem to have answered Finlay's query.

41  Finlay received the address of Augusto de Campos from the Glaswegian poet Edwin Morgan, who introduced Finlay to concrete poetry in May or June 1962. See Greg Thomas, 'Ian Hamilton Finlay, Albert Speer, and the Ideology of the Aesthetic at Little Sparta and Spandau', *Journal of Lusophone Studies*, v/1 (Spring 2020), p. 70.

42  Unpublished letter from Ian Hamilton Finlay to Augusto de Campos, 5 April 1963. Private collection of Augusto de Campos.

43  Unpublished letter from Augusto de Campos to Ian Hamilton Finlay, 1 May 1963, p. 1. Private collection of Augusto de Campos.

44  Unpublished letter from Augusto de Campos to Ian Hamilton Finlay, 30 June 1963. Private collection of Augusto de Campos.

45  Unpublished letter from Augusto de Campos to Ian Hamilton Finlay, 1 May 1963, p. 2. Private collection of Augusto de Campos.

46  Unpublished letter from Ian Hamilton Finlay to Emmett Williams, June 1963, Jean Brown Papers, 890164, Box 55, Getty Research Institute, Los Angeles. Finlay seemed to know more about concrete poetry than he initially let on. For further reading of Finlay's correspondence, please see Stephen Bann's *Midway: Letters from Ian Hamilton Finlay to Stephen Bann, 1964–69* (London, 2014) and his *Stonypath Days: Letters Between Ian Hamilton Finlay and Stephen Bann, 1970–72* (London, 2016).

47  Ian Hamilton Finlay, 'Letters to Ernst Jandl', *Chapman*, 78–9 (1994), p. 12. (Letter dated 1965).

48  Augusto continues: 'Only in the fifties began the rediscovery of Mallarmé, the rediscovery of Pound. Pound suffered at that time from the charge of fascism. His work was very much condemned. We participated in an international movement that tried to rescue Pound, who was excluded from American anthologies.' 'Brazilian Concrete Poetry: How it Looks Today: Haroldo and Augusto de Campos Interviewed by Marjorie Perloff', in *Haroldo de Campos: A Dialogue with the Brazilian Concrete Poet*, ed. K. David Jackson (Oxford, 2005), p. 171.

49  See Antonio Sergio Bessa, 'Sound as Subject: Augusto de Campos's *Poetamenos*', in *The Sound of Poetry / The Poetry of Sound*', pp. 230–31.

50  Rühm, 'The Phenomenon of the "Wiener Gruppe" in the Vienna of the Fifties and Sixties', p. 16.

51 In this anthology, taking the Brazilians as a model, my commentaries on individual poems are predicated on the notion that a glossary of between one and six words enables the English reader to understand the language of the poem. With Japanese concrete poetry, this does not apply since an expert needs to identify and translate the ideographs.

52 Rühm, 'The Phenomenon of the "Wiener Gruppe" in the Vienna of the Fifties and Sixties', p. 20.

53 Marina Corrêa, *Concrete Poetry as an International Movement viewed by Augusto de Campos: An Interview* (São Paulo, 2008).

54 When asked in an interview of 1965 to explain the difference between the avant-garde of today and that of the beginning of the century, Ernst Jandl replied: 'The discovery that the visual poem as well as the sound poem have been effective across linguistic boundaries, that the translation into other languages is scarcely necessary anymore, because the publication of the meaning of two or three words is often sufficient for the understanding of the poem, has strengthened the optimism of the concrete avant-garde.' See Ernst Jandl, 21 November 1965, interview transcribed in the Jandl Nachlass, Österreichen Literaturarchiv, pp. 3–4 (my translation).

55 For Rühm's comments on purifying the German language from the Nazis, see Rühm, 'Konkrete Poesie', p. 37.

56 Jandl and Finlay, *Not a Concrete Pot*, p. 104.

57 See Stephen Bann, *Concrete Poetry: An International Anthology* (London, 1967); Emmett Williams, *An Anthology of Concrete Poetry* (New York, 1967); Eugene Wildman, *Anthology of Concretism* (Chicago, IL, 1967), revd edn (Chicago, IL, 1970); Mary Ellen Solt, *Concrete Poetry: A World View* (Bloomington, IN, 1968).

58 Alex Balgiu and Mónica de la Torre, ed., *Women in Concrete Poetry: 1959–1979* (New York, 2020), pp. 14–17.

59 For a discussion of the post-war periphery, see Marjorie Perloff, *Unoriginal Genius* (Chicago, IL, 2010), p. 61.

60 For this discussion of Haroldo de Campos and Japanese ideograms and of the breaking down of linguistic boundaries in concrete poetry, see John Solt, *Shredding the Tapestry of Meaning: The Poetry and Poetics of Kitasono Katue (1902–1978)* (Cambridge,

MA, 1999), pp. 260–62. Solt quotes Haroldo's term 'universal poetics', from an unpublished letter of 18 March 1979, to Shimizu Toshihiko.

61 See Katue's 'Ocean' and Niikuni's 'River or Sand-bank'. 'Character' and 'ideograph' can be used interchangeably. 'Radical' refers to a meaningful fragment of an ideograph.

62 Philip E. Aarons and Andrew Roth, *In Numbers: Serial Publications by Artists since 1955* (Zurich, 2009), p. 266.

63 For instance, the work of the concrete poets of Scandinavia has recently received serious attention in an important new anthology by the Danish scholar Tania Orum. See *Det ord/ der som et lokomotiv/ traekker en lang vognstamme med sig. – Konkret poesi fra Vagn Steen til i dag* (The word / there like a locomotive / pulls a long wagon trunk with it. – Concrete poetry from Vagn Steen to today)(Grenaa, 2019).

64 Susan Howe has written about concrete poetry, specifically the work of Ian Hamilton Finlay, Eugen Gomringer, Robert Lax and Ad Reinhardt, in her essay 'The End of Art', *Archives of American Art Journal*, XIV/4 (1974).

65 See Nico Vassilakis, 'Finnish vispo: Kokoomateos', *Jacket*, no. 2 (15 February 2016), at https://jacket2.org.

# ACKNOWLEDGEMENTS

This anthology depended, first and foremost, on the collaboration of the following poets, who kindly granted me permission to reproduce their work: Derek Beaulieu, Augusto de Campos, Eugen Gomringer, Susan Howe, Hansjörg Mayer, Franz Mon, Gerhard Rühm, Daniel Spoerri, Andre Vallias. Of these, I must single out Augusto de Campos, whose extraordinary generosity included access to his correspondence with Ian Hamilton Finlay, translations from the Portuguese, and a wealth of research material. Without Augusto, this book would not be what it is today. I also wish to thank Gerhard Rühm, with whom I spent a delightful afternoon at the Christine König Galerie in Vienna. Rühm provided me with books and catalogues, many of which proved to be the heart of my research on the Wiener Gruppe. I am grateful to Susan and Catherine Solt for successfully identifying a marvellous photograph of their mother, Mary Ellen, and to Ann Noël for assisting with the location of Cal Kowal's photographs of Emmett Williams.

During my month-long stay in Vienna in May 2018, I conducted research in the Literature Archive of the Austrian National Library. I wish to thank Bernhard Fetz, Director of both the Literature Archive and the Literature Museum of Vienna, for welcoming me and giving me copies of his publications on Ernst Jandl. Martin Wedl, librarian of the Literature Archive, responded swiftly to all of my requests for archival material. Also in Vienna, Radmila Schweitzer, Director, the Ludwig Wittgenstein Initiative, was a wonderful host and finessed, among other things, a library card which enabled me to work in the reading room of the glorious Hofburg Palace in the city centre.

Among Vienna colleagues, Sylvia Liska graciously introduced me to the Austrian writer Franz Josef Czernin, who shared his essay on 'Poetry. Writing. Picture. Speech' in the work of Heinz Gappmayr. Susanne Neuburger of MUMOK was a stimulating interlocutor on Finlay's installation in the Schweizergarten in Vienna.

I am fortunate to have had the opportunity to work with Michael Leaman, my Publisher. His deep knowledge of concrete poetry and his astute comments on every aspect of my anthology, from selections to scope and balance to definitions, were crucial to the final outcome. At Reaktion Books, I am also grateful to Martha Jay, Managing Editor, and Alex Ciobanu, Assistant to the Publisher, for their excellent work.

Special thanks go to Karen Ehrmann, Permissions Editor, who worked tirelessly and efficiently to secure rights for 134 poems by forty poets and for the images accompanying the introduction. Anyone who has tracked down rights holders knows what an enormous task it is to identify the contact information, negotiate the terms and organize the data. Karen's help was invaluable.

Among friends and colleagues, I wish to extend heartfelt thanks to poet, translator and scholar John Solt, author of the definitive Anglophone study of the Japanese poet Kitasono Katue. John taught me how to read and interpret the ideographs of Kitasono and Seiichi Niikuni and how to understand them in the context of the concrete poetry movement. Without his help, the Japanese presence in this anthology might have been scarce. For stimulating exchanges about concrete poetry, I am also grateful to Sergio Bessa, Craig Dworkin and Wendy Salmond.

My colleagues at the Getty have helped and supported this project in many ways. I wish especially to thank Marcia Reed, chief curator, Glenn Phillips, head of modern and contemporary collections, and Zanna Gilbert, senior research specialist, for our productive conversations about concrete poetry. Lauren Graber, my research assistant, applied her German expertise to the translation of unpublished documents and interviews and assisted skilfully with the biographies and the dating of individual poems.

Lastly, a great debt goes to my husband, Robert Lempert, a senior scientist and policy analyst, and to my mother, Marjorie Perloff, a literary critic. Rob's remarkable skills in logic and clarity of reasoning helped enormously with the challenging task of organizing the introduction, and his good company lifted my spirits throughout. As a concrete poetry scholar who introduced me to Augusto de Campos in São Paulo, my mother encouraged the anthology from the beginning and became another pair of eyes (and ears), especially with the Wiener Gruppe, a natural for her owing to her Viennese heritage. She took me to task when an analysis fell short and never failed to remind me of my audience. Thanks to her insight, Finlay's poem 'To the Painter Juan Gris' with its 'Happy Apple' text, will never look the same.

# PHOTO ACKNOWLEDGEMENTS

The editor and publishers wish to express their thanks to the below sources of illustrative material and/or permission to reproduce it. Every effort has been made to contact copyright holders; should there be any we have been unable to reach or to whom inaccurate acknowledgements have been made please contact the publishers, and full adjustments will be made to any subsequent printings. Unless indicated otherwise, all photos provided courtesy of the Getty Research Institute, Los Angeles:

Used by permission of Jeremy Adler: pp. 130–31; © 2021 Carl Andre/ Licensed by VAGA at Artists Rights Society (ARS), NY, photos © The Museum of Modern Art (MOMA), New York, licensed by Scala, Florence/Art Resource, NY: pp. 176–7, 178; photos courtesy Derek Beaulieu, used by permission: p. 192; used by permission of the Bob Cobbing Estate: pp. 132, 133; © Claus Bremer, photo Franz J. Wamhof/© Zentrum für Kunst und Medien (ZKM), Karlsruhe: p. 163; from John Cage, *Silence: Lectures and Writings* (Middletown, CT, 1961), © 1961 John Cage, reprinted with permission of Wesleyan University Press, Middletown, CT: pp. 179, 180, 181; © Augusto de Campos: pp. 45, 46, 47, 48–9, 50, 51, 52–3, 54 (photo courtesy Augusto de Campos), 55 (photo courtesy Augusto de Campos), 56, 57 (additional permission courtesy Anabela Plaza), 58, 59, 60 (photo courtesy Augusto de Campos), 61; © Ivan de Campos: pp. 97, 98, 99, 100, 101; courtesy Jan De Vree: p. 174; © Dieter Roth Estate, courtesy Hauser & Wirth: pp. 17, 150, 151, 152–3, 154, 155, 156, 157; © Edgard Braga Estate: p. 96; © The Estate of bpNichol: p. 182;